The motive power depot on the 4mm scale layout of the Skipton & District MRS. Note the coaling stage at the top of the photograph while the loco shed is at the bottom right.
/ Brian Monaghan

£2.95

BATHAMPTON
460

Model Railway Constructor ANNUAL

Edited by S.W. Stevens-Stratten

£2.00
2020
10/5

LONDON

IAN ALLAN LTD

First published 1978

ISBN 0 7110 0864 7

Published by Ian Allan Ltd, Shepperton, Surrey; and printed in the United Kingdom by Ian Allan Printing Ltd

Contents

Previous page: *GWR No 6026* King John *on the 11.45 Bristol-Paddington express passes slowly through Bathampton station on the 4mm scale layout of G. Mawson.*
/ Brian Monaghan

Left: *A 4mm scale model of an LMSR 2-6-0 'Crab' No 2716 passing over a realistic country roadbridge.*
/ Brian Monaghan

Introduction

Although the *Model Railway Constructor* has been published regularly since 1934, this is the first time an Annual has been issued, and we trust it will become a popular and regular publication each year. It may interest readers to know that in 1951 two smaller additional publications were issued in mid-Summer and Christmas called *Model Railway Constructor Special* which contained articles and photographs which for reasons of length, available space, interest or just 'the Editor's whim' were omitted from the normal monthly issues. For many diverse reasons the idea was not continued, but now with the greater interest in the model railway hobby, the idea has been resurrected and we trust it will give you pleasure.

With 12 different scales and gauges from Z gauge to gauge 1, not including the Narrow Gauge deviations, it is not always possible to include something for every scale, and therefore only the more popular ones can be covered, but ideas described for one scale are often equally suitable, albeit sometimes with a minor modification, to the scale of your choice. A large number of useful hints and tips can be gained by reading articles on another scale or system.

We have deliberately not included items dealing with the building of kits or the conversion of proprietary items, for it may well be that by the time the article appears in print, the kit or commercial item may not be on the market! Such items, we feel, are best left to the pages of the monthly magazine where they are more topical. Similarly this Annual does not include reviews of equipment which is a feature for which the *Model Railway Constructor* is noted, as it gives unbiased reports on new items produced both by the leading manufacturers and the smaller producers of kits and components.

Four of the photo-features included within these covers are the work of Brian Monaghan, a photographer of international repute, whose excellent photographs in black and white and in colour, regularly grace the pages of *Model Railway Constructor.*

The work of at least three model railway clubs is featured here, which shows the scope of large layouts which can be built with the aid of many enthusiasts working together for a common cause. The benefits of club membership is not confined to the construction and operation of layouts, for much knowledge can be assimilated at club meetings and there is usually a specialist who can solve a problem or assist a newcomer to the hobby. With over 340 model railway clubs in the UK, there is one in most large towns.

Finally, we would like to point out that the article "South for Moonshine" although written by the Editor, does not depict his own layout. It is the layout of a friend, the late Lewis Carroll, who gave the Editor many notes and jottings during his many visits. The article has been written in the hope that it will encourage others towards more prototypical operation and that some of the novel yet highly successful ideas can be perpetuated, which would have been the wish of the builder.

S. W. Stevens-Stratten,
Epsom

Pipe Dreams

L. G. SWAN

As with most small boys, I had had a model railway from an early age: just when I cannot remember. As was the form in those days — the early-mid '30s — my layout started as a Hornby O gauge layout. The 0-4-0 tender engine was, as one realises now, hopefully numbered 5600 and was red, which I suppose must have set the seal on my predeliction for the LMSR. This in itself was strange, for we lived in South London and it was not until an Aunt moved to Kettering late in the '30s that I can ever remember travelling on the LMSR, although I can clearly remember visiting the exhibition at Euston in 1937 and going over the 'Coronation' and 'Silver Jubilee'. Yet on the other hand my Grandfather was a driver on the SECR and subsequently the Southern, and we went almost every year to Swanage by rail.

Be that as it may, tin-plate O gauge it was, clockwork, ('we' didn't like electricity) 2ft radius curves and all! It was added to gradually — money was not easily come by, and there was education to think of too. Instead of an Easter Egg one year, I had a No 1 tank No 2120. The two high spots, however, were a new Bassett-Lowke 0-6-0, No 4256 super detailed by my father, and weighted, which pulled everything I ever owned, and the Hornby Compound No 1185. This engine was second hand with a badly painted '4.P' in gold on the cab side sheets. But to me it looked superb and went like the wind. In retrospect, one wonders how these locos and coaches managed to keep on the rails, rushing round 2ft radius curves over none too level drawing room circuit. But they did, and gave endless hours of enjoyment to child and parent alike!!

Other items during this era included a Bing 0-4-0 tender loco (L&NWR livery No 326), a home built diesel 0-4-0 No 7100, a variety of rolling stock which increased by the odd one or two every birthday and Christmas. Eventually, I had six LMSR 4-wheeled coaches made up in two rakes of three, 'Pines Express' or 'Comet', a 4 wheeled Pullman (probably given by a relation who didn't know any better!), a Bing coach with opening doors, (fascinating) painted LMSR (unlined) by my father, and an assorted collection of vans and wagons. On the home-built side, there was a 3-coach articulated unit, which with the compound formed the pride of the line. For a number of reasons the War prevented the completion of four projects. One was a red 2-6-0 'Crab' allocated No 2945(!) (almost completed but not quite) another, a Pug (to my scale drawings) the third, a Scot (to be rebuilt by me from a discarded Hornby 'Flying Scotsman') and last, a Watford Oerlikon unit, the suspension difficulties of the clockwork motor proving the stumbling block here.

Also killed by the War was the move and completion of the layout to the loft.

Over this period, I recall the Twin Trix layouts and the introduction of the three-rail Hornby-Dublo system. Both of these were sumarally dismissed by the household as looking like powered worms.

Inevitably as the years passed the children left home. With the sudden death of my father, the house became too much of a burden to my mother and it was sold. Due to my nomadic existence all the O gauge railway was sold too. Yet only some two years were to pass before I took up active model railwaying again.

At the end of 1960 I found myself at the age of 32 having to study again. Now with a young family of two and the level of some subjects being in the order of 'inter B.Sc +' I found things quite a strain. Fortunately there were a number of fellow sufferers. One of them, Jim Allison, was (I soon found out) a model railway enthusiast and we soon began to spend our free time — what there was of it — talking railways and looking at his single line terminus base-boards. Dare I admit that even during some of the duller lectures (and there were some) we resorted to tabulating points for and against Webb, the latest white-metal kit, or end-to-end v circuit layouts. Add to this that we were near Swindon, Jim was a Southern/GWR fan, plastic models were on the market, and it will be realised the time was ripe for the rebirth of railway interest. At this time too, I had my family in the wing of an old Vicarage — flag-stone floors and huge rooms. This is of relevence to this story, as I was allocated a large room for a study. In it my first models and base-boards were made.

As I have observed, Kitmaster and Airfix 4mm scale kits were on the market. My first two locomotive kits were a 'Duchess' and the 'Pug'. From the first I wanted these motorised, and Jim allowed me running rights in order to test the final products. I also purchased a cement and an oil wagon on the rolling stock side. While these were in hand two things took place which had a considerable effect on my

Right: *A completed K's kit of a CR 0-4-4T No 445 fitted with K's Mk1 motor and flywheel. Extra detail includes PC Models number plates and painted in St Rollox blue by John Carter. Weighted to 15½oz.*

Below: *A completed K's kit of a LNWR 0-6-2T coal tank No 252. K's motor and extra detail including nickel-silver cab roof, guard irons, sand pipes, reversing rod, front steps, and PC Models number plates, safety valve rod etc. Weighted to 12oz and painted by John Carter.*

Bottom: *BR Drewry 0-6-0 shunter. Airfix kit body on handbuilt chassis with Tri-ang motor and Hamblings wheels. Weighted to 8¼oz.*

subsequent modelling. The first was reading in the Model Press of Mr Jack Newton's article on Proportional Power Classifications, and the second, a visit to Mr Newton in Bristol. It was purely fortuitous I was in the area — it was the first and last time — and called on the off chance. He and his wife made me most welcome and although packing up for a move, the stud of locos ouilt to a standard specification were brought out and shown me. Top secret at the time was his twin-engined chassis for a BR Class 9F: a beautiful job, which had me enthralled.

Meanwhile, my pipe-dream stud had been compiled. I think it contained nine locomotives, and included a Class 9F, parallel boiler Scot; Compound; 0-6-0 4 F; and MR 0-4-4T. I had become completely out of touch with railway matters. On reading model and rail magazines I began to realise my short list contained incompatabilities: for instance parallel Scots were all rebuilt and Compounds were no more. If I ever built the locos I liked, there would be a most odd mixture of eras. I was increasing my knowledge of railway history, reading Nock, Tuplin and Hamilton Ellis. I gradually began to formulate the idea of three basic eras so that the locos could conform to one or the other of them. This idea has crystallised into the present concept of Regrouping circa 1904-1913; LMSR, 1935-1939; and BR, 1958-1962. This took some time for me to formulate.

During this period I had found out what the model trade had to offer. I bought a Hornby Dublo Class 8F 2-8-0 and partly detailed it — vacuum pipes, front steps, fined off the reversing rod, glazed the window,

Above: *GWR 4-6-0 No 5034* Corfe Castle. *Hornby Dublo body and tender on a handbuilt chassis with Tri-ang motor mounted on the rear of chassis driving on the centre axle. Body has extra detail. Painted by R. Denny.*

Araldited a piece of rail on the motion plate across the crosshead guides, also Araldited correct wheel weights, and replaced the pony truck wheels. She was repainted in LMSR colours, and numbered 8147. A BR 2-6-4T was purchased and similarly detailed, but not repainted, of course, or renumbered. Of kits, the K's CR 0-4-4T was bought, and the bodyline MR 0-6-0T. Both were professionally painted and numbered 445 and 1940 respectively. The BR stud was increased with a Kitmaster Class 9F (tender motor) a Class 4MT Mogul (Tri-ang chassis) and a Tri-ang *Britannia*. This latter was super detailed with metal smoke deflectors, hand-rails, and regulator rodding, plastic ATC box, various pipes, tender axle-box covers and vacuum pipe. The bogie steps were cut off and Araldited under the running plate along with the front vacuum pipe. The chassis was completely re-wheeled, correct slide-bars built up on a saddle to fit behind the cylinders, and piston and crossheads made to fit the fined-down connecting and coupling rods. The engine was then weighted, numbered 70033, named *Charles Dickens,* matt varnished, dirtied, and finally out-shopped with glazed cab. This last rebuild marked an important step in my modelling as it was the first time I made and soldered parts: up to then I had used adhesives with filed metal or plastic pieces.

It is worthwhile here to take a slightly retrospective look at my loco specification. Generally I wanted to conform to Mr Newton's policy, but of course as a non-scratch builder at this stage and dependent basically on kits this was not possible. I did weight the engines in relation to their power classifications (ie $1/3$ adhesion weight in ounces). I did as much detailing as I think can be reasonably seen and without being too fragile. In this context as an example I do not consider brake rodding 'on', except for such prototypes as the Midland 0-6-0T or Bulleid Pacifics, and brake hangers and shoes fill me with fear! Wheels need to be scale size or slightly smaller (the over-scale flanges making up for the odd fraction of a mm), the correct number of spokes is not high on my priority list, but weights for the drivers are (tooth-paste tube and Araldite). As for couplings, I tried A-Z at first, but found them not reliable after a train had been reversed, so went nap on Hornby. If space permits eventually, I will use my own 3-link or screw couplings — I say space as this will require minimum radii of about 4ft. The gauge is 16.5mm as quite frankly at the formative period I was somewhat put off by the EM, EEM, and 19mm boys and took the line of least resistance — or simplest construction.

The general requirements for a track plan were being roughed out in concert with rolling stock needs. I thought the best I could hope for would be a room/hut/garage of between 12-16ft long and 8-10ft wide (and still do!). I wanted to run express passenger trains with 8-12 coaches, minerals of similarly realistic length. Short of going out into the garden (now a possibility with plastic based track I suppose) an end-

Top right: *The component parts — bodywork for loco and tender and chassis for both. The backplate of the loco is made of lead; the tender built for 8thou nickel-silver sheet on a 10thou base.*

Centre right: *An L&YR Aspinall 4-4-2 takes shape. A new feature for my models is a tender pick-up to overcome loss of current through the very close-coupled drivers.*

Below: *LMSR 'Royal Scot' class 4-6-0 No 6166* London Rifle Brigade. *This is a home built loco with a Tri-ang motor front mounted. The model has a Hornby Dublo tender with fitted handrails, shovel plate etc. PC Models name and smokebox number plate. Weighted to 21¼oz and painted by John Carter.*

to-end layout seemed impossible. My sketches gradually developed into two twin tracked circuits. The last drawing shows a station on one side with the necessary crossovers, a single road terminal, and a small yard and engine shed. The lines disappear into tunnels as they curve away either side of the station, the slow pair climbing up and eventually over the fast lines on the opposite side of the layout. On this side both circuits are virtually hidden to avoid the tail-chasing aspect of continuous runs. However off the slow lines a single line runs to a small terminus. Under the cover both circuits have waiting loops, three for each line. The idea here is that the trains of the three eras can be held and at any point in time I can run a complete pre-grouping, LMSR, or BR system. While at the Vicarage a start was made on this scheme.

The layout was started (inevitably!) on the station side. Base-boards were made of Weyroc with 1in by 2in outside framing to the 4ft by 2ft panels. Virtually the whole of the station side of the track was laid, but no scenic effects were made. The track was mainly Welcut with fibre base points, but I soon began to make my own point-work to enable the layout more realistically to conform in the space available. I also tried the Little Western method of track assembly. In all cases the sleepers were glued to thin cork strip (from the local garage) which itself had previously been stuck to the Weyroc. Peco ballast was sprinkled over the track while the glue was wet, and the surplus brushed off later. Bases were aligned by 2in hinges with removable hinge-pins, and stood on 5/8in pipe legs threaded to screw into metal roses. Locknuts held the legs tight once the base-boards had been levelled. The aim of this method of support was three-fold: to allow small floor irregularities to be taken up, to allow the supports to be removed easily and stowed in clips under the boards, and to reduce overall weight. The set of boards was designed to stack in slotted angle for storage — which is where the layout has been for five years now! So when I return to UK I will be able to give a full report on the durability of my methods on construction. But one lives and learns of course. This form of construction made a very noisey track, the cork providing little if any dampening. Points were worked by tubing as I expected this to be positive and cheap. I now consider the saving to be marginal, and with the problems of remote control and base-board crossing I would use motors for any future work — rebuilding and new. From the point of view of realism, I spoilt the station layout by using straight roads for the through platforms. There were reasons for this, but it would look much better to have had the lines gently curving. I worked to a minimum radius of 30in on the fast, and 24in for the slow and yard tracks. However there were one or two sharper curves I must admit, the Tal-y-llyn curves as Jim called them, by the sites of the coal staithes and goods depot.

I have mentioned the use of passing (or waiting) loops, and so it is now logical to consider the train types I would run. I plan on five basic types, one each for the up and down fast and slow, and the single line working, as follows: express passenger, mineral, stopping passenger or parcels, stopping freight, and the local 'crab-and-winkle'. Rolling stock takes second priority over locomotive construction due to movement and space, but several rakes have been completed, and items for others collected.Thus the BR express, mineral (Airfix tankers), parcels and freight (various makes), and local (Exley) are complete. The LMSR express (Exley) and stopping freight are complete also. The mineral was going to consist of the Airfix steel wagon, and I had completed this train in grey livery (with A-Z couplings) for the 2-8-0, when my final rationalisation of periods ruled out their use, I found out the colour was wrong, and the couplings became obsolescent. Such is progress! The wagons will now join the BR era, suitably repainted, renumbered, and recoupled, and in their place must come plank wagons. Here I may be able to employ some of the new PO series. The pre-Grouping stock will be the greatest problem. Of the four main companies — LNWR, MR, L&YR, and CR, — I already have six K's six-wheel coaches (three as yet unpainted) and one bogie representing the LNWR, a Midland bogie (Exley, as is the LNWR), and two Tri-ang CR coaches. These latter are to be remodelled with flat ends and K's bogies.With nothing representing the L&YR, and very little in the way of goods stock, much work needs to be done.

With track and stock coming along well at the Vicarage, my next move entailed the storage of the base-boards and all the then-completed rolling stock. I retained all my locos as fortunately Jim Allison moved to the same area, and our houses were within a short walking distance of each other. Thus track-nights were still possible for he was able to set up his layout in a spare room that he now had. Indeed with only a little goading from me he developed his line rather anti-Beechingly so that not only could a train be run out of the station as far as the throat, the original limit of his line, but round on a complete two-track circuit. His single line terminus thus became a two-road through station — still somewhere in the West of England — with at times one of the busiest services in the British Isles, including London Bridge. Indeed it could be likened to Carlisle, for as time went by through it ran not only his stud of locos — Bulleid Pacifics, NI, M7, R1, Castle, Pannier, and Prairie, but my Precursor, George, Claughton, Coal tank, a Johnson big 0-6-0T, CR 0-4-4T, Scot, Crab, 8F, Britannia, 4MT mogul and tank, 9F, Co-Bo, Drewry 0-6-0, and Castle. As

Top right: *LNWR 'Claughton' class 4-6-0* Ralph Brocklebank.*Another handbuilt loco with Tri-ang motor driving on cente axle. Weighted to 19¼oz. Painted by John Carter.*

Centre right: *L&YR 4-4-2 'Highflyer' No 1406. Another handbuilt model with Tri-ang motor. Hamblings wheels and weighted to 12½oz. The K's tender axleboxes were cast from a home made pattern.*

Bottom right: *LNWR 4-4-0 'Precursor' No 643* Sirocco. *This was my first completely handmade model fitted with Tri-ang motor and wheels by Hamblings (drivers) and Nucro and Jackson. The model is weighted to 12oz.*

Below: *LNWR 4-4-0 'George' No 1800* Coronation. *A handbuilt body and chassis fitted with a K's Mk1 motor and weighted to 13oz. The model represents Works No 5000 as slightly modified with front sandboxes on the running plates and no dust guards.*

some of these were to be seen in chassis form, then in natural metal finish (no workshop grey for us) before blossoming out in correct livery, the cavalcade to a 4mm scale enthusiast standing on one of the platforms must have seemed quite remarkable!

The move had one good effect on my modelling: I bought a Unimat lathe and vertical drill. With this installed I immediately set to work to build my first loco. Not an inside cylinder tank like any sensible chap, but a twin-motored, Walschaert-valved 2-10-0 to replace the plastic model — shades of Jack Newton again. Construction followed his earlier articles, and gave little trouble other than being unable to make the two Tri-ang motors behave together. So the 9F became single engined, and works well. Suitably dirtied it took the road as 90250, the last steam loco built at Crewe, weighing 21oz (still a little shy of weight, but I can't find any more room) and flanged as on the prototype. My first effort, I am still pleased with it although the valve link brackets could be improved. The tender is a modified Tri-ang with bearing cups and metal wheels. This brings out a point that I decided quite early on, namely that if suitable items existed on the market I would use them. I personally find time is in short supply, indeed months go by when I am unable to do any modelling at all. At my present rate of construction it will take 12 years to complete my stud! Thus I would rather buy an item than make it providing it looks, or can be made to look, the part. This applies equally to complete models as to components. Thus I will use a bought turned or cast part on a basically home built loco, a tender (as on the 9F, Castle, and Scot), a boiler (Dublo Castle and A4), or buy a complete kit such as the Wills 4F or K's Spinner.

Cheered by the success of the 9F, I presented the Kitmaster 9F to Jim — it carried a number from the S&D allocation, so was quite in keeping with his track. I then started to fill in the many spaces in my stud list. The LNW Precursor was completely hand built, then a Castle chassis for the Hornby-Dublo body and tender, a chassis for the Airfix Drewry shunter, Scot No 6166 with Hornby-Dublo Stanier tender, Claughton No 1159 complete, and finally before having to move again, the LNWR George 'Coronation'. This latter was produced as a control to run against *Sirocco* to compare motor performances. All my previous home-built models had Tri-ang 3-pole motors.To 'Coronation' I fitted a K's Mk1 5-pole. In point of fact I have been unable adequately to compare these engines as I have not had access to a suitable track since they left the paint shops. Being a firm believer that a good model can be ruined by bad painting, and a poor model considerably improved, I have had the LNWR, CR, MR, Scot and Crab locos painted by a specialist. The Castle was painted by R. Denny. While the home built details were in hand I completed a Wills Class 4F as No 4256 with the Wills chassis modified to conform to the general specification. I also purchased two Hornby-Dublo Metrovick Co-Bos, to which I added some chassis details, disc codes, and painted them to conform one to 1958, the other to 1962, livery.

Another move has severely limited my modelling activities. I am constructing an Aspinall Highflyer, but in two years have only completed chassis, tender top, cab and firebox details. However I have finished a MR Spinner, No 123, and am currently trying to make a runner out of a Fowler Class 3P kit — this to become eventually LMSR No 1. Frames have been marked, drilled, and cut for a Compound (which may have a Jackson superstructure, but home-made Deeley tender), and a Fowler Class 3F 0-6-0T.

This then is the state of the game at the moment. I have already discussed lessons from my track building efforts but what of the loco construction over the past

Below: *MR 4-2-2 'Spinner' No 123. A K's kit with a Mk1 motor fitted in the tender. Extra detail includes sanding pipes and filler covers, dome spring valve stems, cab roof, reversing wheel, handbrake, guard irons etc. Painted by John Carter.*

five years? First, given a minimum of tools any 4mm model can be built, but that minimum must include a good vertical drilling machine, and if possible a lathe. Secondly in order to avoid annealing, and hard work in filing and cutting, it is better to use the thinnest possible material consistant with it's 'handleability'. As an example I have always cut frames from 1/16th nickel-silver strip. I will try 1/32in on the next chassis, although I may have to use K's bushes to reduce side-play. I started using 10thou nickel-silver sheet for smokebox, boiler, and firebox details. I now use a mixture of 8thou and 5thou. There is always the temptation to improve the breed — subsequent locos having more detail than the one before as knowledge and ability is gained. This I have tried to avoid: the basic concept for *Coronation* was the same as for the 9F. There are no more details although the component parts may be finer. The only thing I would like to add is some form of lateral control to bogie trucks, especially of 4-4-0s. I have yet to see or read of a simple design which achieves this without affecting the riding or pulling characteristics.

Of the kits, I have nothing but praise for the old Kitmaster and Airfix series (the former have ceased production and some of their range has been taken over by the latter). I think they did much to improve our hobby. The detail included in the plastic was superb and I like to think it acted as a spur to the other manufacturers. The white metal kits are good too — as indeed they should be at the price. I have stopped thinking (or hoping) they will be easy to assemble. A square, and easy running kit is as hard to achieve as a hand built one — often more so in fact as something broken or out of square can not be simply resoldered. One item on a metal kit I now invariably replace is the scale 4in thick roof with a piece of 8thou or 5thou nickel-silver sheet.

I have outlined improvements I would make to the track survey and point control. The noise level is a snag which as I see it could only be really overcome by scrapping the 'portable' approach, and employing a good sound and solid base. Whether felt or foam plastic under the Weyroc would deaden the noise to any great extent is doubtful. To lay track on expanded polystyrene is tempting, but thin strips of this could so easily distort during handling, and what would happen to it with 20oz plus locos pounding over it I dread to think.

Needless to say, I have names for the stations, and have photo spotted real buildings and features to which the eventual layout will try to conform. For those who like to identify a layout with a particular area, I can say the through station is Newton Dale, in the hilly country south-east of Carlisle. A Midland station, it is situated on a LNWR-MR joint line, the valley carrying not only the Midland road, but also the LNWR alternative loop to the West Coast line. From the station runs the LNWR-MR-L&YR-CR joint branch line to the coast (in a manner similar to the Portpatrick and Wigtown branch), the station Port Lune being fashioned after the G&SWR Kirkcudbright station. Newton Dale traffic is mainly through, although a small amount of both goods and passenger is worked for the nearby village of Newton Tony. Transfer and connecting traffic occurs between the LNWR and MR lines, and in season there is very heavy holiday traffic to Port Lune. This line was well used at the turn of the century, the resort being particularly popular with the North Country and Glasgow folk, and happily this was still so in 1962 (when the clock stopped for this layout). During both Wars various Service establishments maintained the need for the branch, indeed the Civil Engineer had to ensure quite heavy trains could use the line, and since 1917 quite large locomotives have been able to work to the coast.

With the scene so unmistakably LMSR how is it I have mentioned a Castle and an A4? For various reasons I want to run a Schools (*Dulwich*), Bulleid West Country (*Swanage*), and Castle (*Corfe Castle*). And so I decided to include in my stud some famous classes from other Groups. Thus in addition to those just mentioned, I hope to have *Mallard,* perhaps a V2, and a Marsh Atlantic (*Peveril Point*) running over the metals. Their role — well, excursions, trials, preservation runs, Society tours... I'll think of something!

Postscript

Since the start of my own stud, railway books have been printed in ever increasing numbers. It is interesting to contemplate a stud based on might-have-beens. E. S. Cox has written several books now in which sufficient data exists in line form for some enterprising chap to build a full range of motive power — Garratts, Compounds and Simples from 0-4-0ST to eight-coupled passengers and freights. If the details do not attract, then one could become CME and produce one's own chimney etc profiles. The building of freelance models, with their own special livery, seems to have died out, yet was very popular pre '39. Perhaps this facet of our hobby will be reborn with the demise of British steam.

Right: *A 'Crab' 2-6-0 No 2716 drifts across bridge 17A over Bickering Beck as it heads a stopping train into Much Bickering. Thunder clouds gather in the background and heavy rain has fallen on the moors judging by the amount of water in the Beck.*

2716
L M S

Much Bickering

The 4mm scale layout of the Newport MRS

A. BENNETT

Introduction

I suppose that most model railways are built to replace older, less satisfactory layouts. Much Bickering was no exception to this rule, and was constructed to replace an ailing model based on Chepstow and Barry Island. This previous layout was built in a room approx 12ft by 10ft, and on Club nights things became very congested. As a result it was decided to sweep away Chepstow & Barry and to build anew. Four completely conventional flat topped 4ft by 2ft baseboards were built, and on this was going a Fiddle — station — Fiddle layout, with one Fiddle yard operator being out in the corridor because obviously the layout was too long for the room. To make matters considerably worse, our neighbours in the room above us were of the joy through strength brigade, and the crashes on the ceiling as they dropped their bar-bells and other pieces of iron was, we thought, good neither for the ceiling, nor our layout, bare boards though it was.

We were fortunate in that the opportunity of new premises came our way, so we moved into the first floor of a near derelict church hall and had nearly 48ft by 20ft of clear space to play with. This space in itself caused some problems because with such a large amount of room in which to spread ourselves layout design and standards were of vital importance.

Eventually two layouts were proposed, one Universal OO Gauge and the other Finescale OO. The Universal layout does not really concern us here, however, it may be mentioned that when built it was of the free standing L-girder kind. It is now no longer with us, but then, neither is Much Bickering for that matter.

For the so called fine-scale layout we next needed a trackplan to work from, and a suitable one was found by one of our members. Apparently, in the course of its wanderings through the nether parts of Yorkshire, the Whitby and Pickering line passes through Goathland, an attractive, if austere, stone built station, typical of the area. This unsuspecting place was chosen as the prototype of the layout, and a suitable trackplan copying all the salient features was drawn. Models of the finished layout were produced, everyone dutifully admired them so with the confidence of enthusiasm we took our four bare baseboards, got out the soldering irons and track gauges and prepared to sign a few cheques. The layout was on its way.

Left: *The approach to Much Bickering. A 'Crab' No 42715 fusses through with a van train while a rebuilt 'Scot' rushes down the gradient hauling some Eastern Region stock. A Class 2P 4-4-0 waits in the siding.*

Below: *Goathland in the summer of 1900, the prototype on which the model is based.*

Fig 1

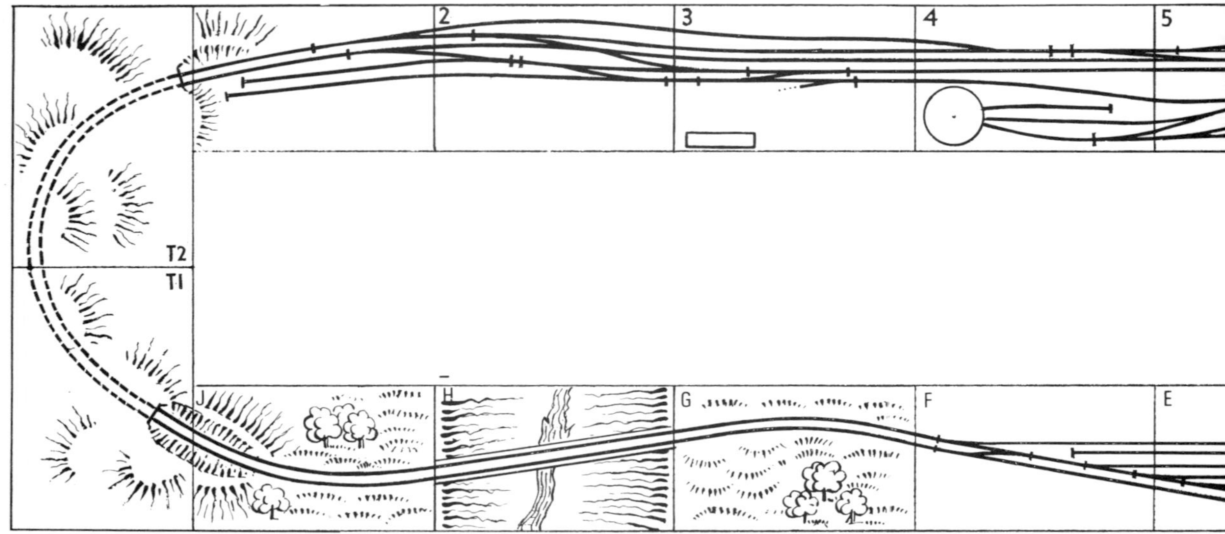

Baseboards

Anyone with sense would agree that there is an easy way, and a hard way, of doing anything. In retrospect it seems as though we did everything the hard way. Take the baseboards we had as an example. When they were assembled in the usual manner with coach bolts, folding legs, etc and we then tried to draw on them the track plan of Goathland, we found that there was not sufficient width. Instead of doing the easy thing, and the sensible thing, which would be to reconsider the track plan, we decided to alter all the baseboards because another consideration had to be taken into account as well. The prototype itself was not built on the flat: not only did its mainline have a gradient, but its sidings wandered vertically up and down. Well now, if there is one thing a flat baseboard cannot do easily it is portray vertical depth. Height can always be built up, but depth — never.

Our actions to cure these faults resulted in the curious name of the layout. (Your can draw your own conclusions about the derivation of the name of the present layout — Long Suffren). Effectively the baseboards were completely rebuilt, with outriggers providing the extra width, and cleats and risers giving the extra height. The baseboard top material, ½in Weyroc, was changed to open top construction, and after the track plan had been drawn on and the outline cut, we found that it could be eased into the correct gradients and screwed to the cleats. Reference to illustrations show how the layout timberwork is constructed, and how the various boards are held together. Over the years 1968-72, when this layout was available for public display, the baseboards held up to the rigours of travel and erection quite well, but they did have certain disadvantages which have been largely overcome in our latest effort.

Trackwork

If you are still with us, and are not forcing yourself to remain awake, try to conjure up before your mind's eye the layout as it has up to now been described. If you cannot visualise it, look at the illustration, ignore the trackwork and you have it.

The centre line of the track run was the next thing to be tackled. The flowing curves were drawn quite easily by marking four or five positions of the centre line accurately, and then joining the points with a long wooden lath. The proper curve could then be drawn using the lath as a guide — fig 2. If I remember, the lath we used was about 10ft long. Obviously the lath has to be quite flexible, otherwise when fixing siding C/L, or other sharpish 'bends' it could snap.

These carefully plotted and drawn lines were now used as guide lines for laying the track underlay. This material, was ¼in cork flooring tiles, which was cut up into strips ¾in wide.

Now it is obvious that a line, however carefully drawn, is going to be pretty useless if you are going to slap underlay all over it, so we used the line as a guide to lay the cork strip — first on one side of it, then on the other — fig 3. Working this way meant that the centre line was still marked as the join between strips. Because the strips had a rubber/cork base they could also be bent around the curves used. The underlay for

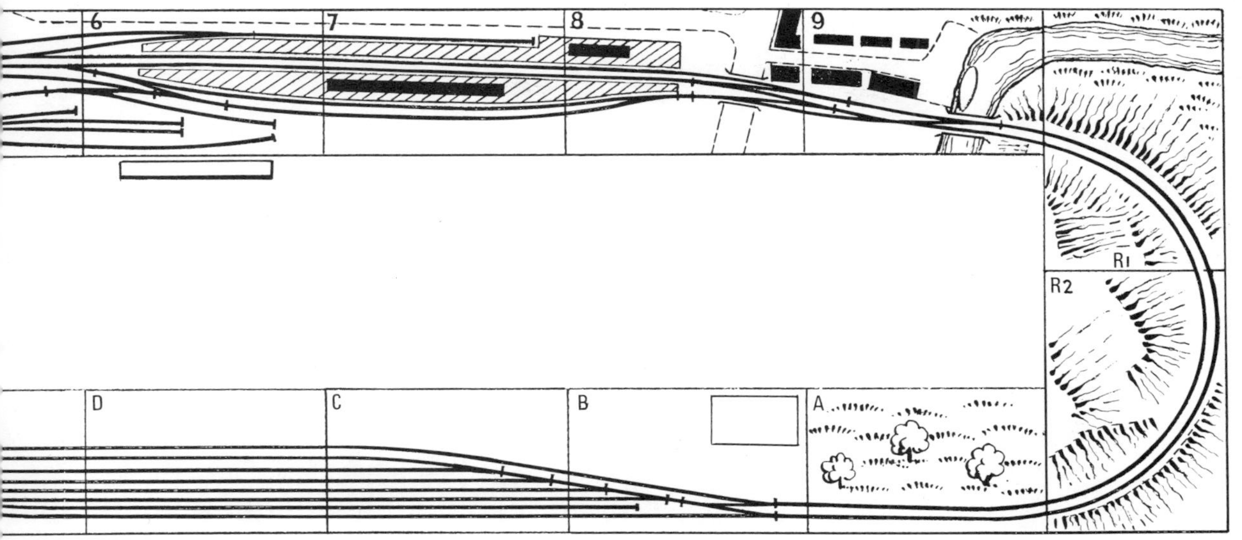

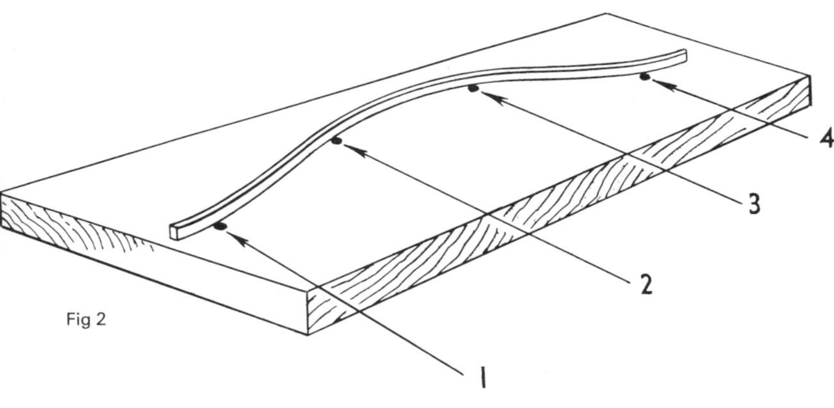

Fig 2

Left: *Method for drawing accurate track centre lines. 1, 2, 3 and 4 are accurately marked points joined by a wooden lath. Flowing curves marked in with pencil.*

Below left: *Method showing how to preserve track centre line when laying underlay. A-B is trackwork c/line. Strips of cork are laid either side. XY is join between cork strips, but still shows c/line.*

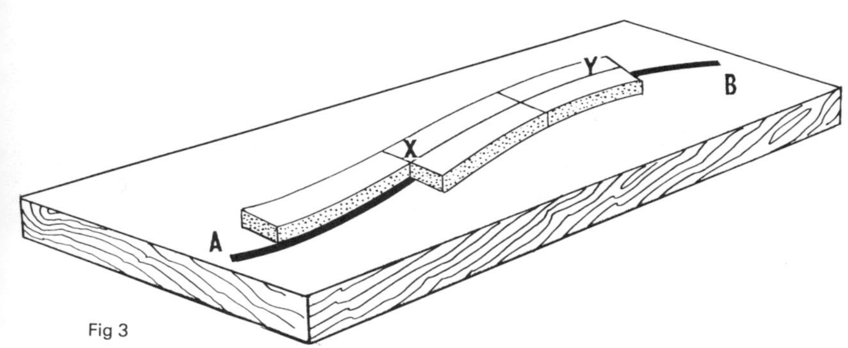

Fig 3

the complete layout was stuck down in this way using Evo-stik, and after the glue had stuck, all the cork was sanded down with an orbital sander, and chamfers cut to represent the shoulders of the ballast.

From the very beginning we had determined that the layout would have hand built trackwork to BRMSB OO gauge standards and this was the next thing to be tackled. One of our members managed to produce a half track jig, milled out of solid aluminium, which provided correct sleeper spacings — including the slight narrowing of the spaces at the end of each 60ft (scale) of rail — and which enabled us to produce halftrack from copper laminate sleepers soldered to Dead Scale Bull Head rail. The half track was lifted from the jig and relaid in its correct position on the layout; with drawing pins holding everything in place; then with the aid of a roller gauge, the second rail was soldered into position. Point work was also club built using jig built standardised crossings — 1 in 7, I think, although the length of the point could vary according to its site.

When a certain section of trackwork had been completed in this way, it was lifted — points as well — and placed on the floor. Because we had been using an acid flux, it was thoroughly washed with a weak solution of washing soda and then swilled down with freshwater and allowed to dry. Earlier, we had found that the narrow saw cut in the centre of the copper on the sleeper providing the necessary insulation was sometimes not doing its job properly and short circuits would appear when under test. To cure these short circuits meant opening out each sawcut with a needle file — not a job enjoyed by many, and even then results could vary because slivers of swarf could cause short circuits again. To speed up the process, therefore, our club electrician turned up one evening with a piece of apparatus which could kick out a few hundred volts under controlled conditions, and when this was attached to the track we most effectively burned away the swarf and cleared the short circuits. I can well remember seeing this machine at work, when one evening we attached the wire to the track we had first cleaned — and dried — and switched off the lights. When the machine was turned on, the trackwork under test sparkled with pin points of light which gradually diminished in number until eventually none were to be seen. Everyone of those pin points was a potential short circuit at 12V, but a definite short at 300V. Needless to say, after the introduction of this short circuit tester we had few problems caused by copper swarf. Nowadays of course, a healthy 1/8in gap is milled out of the sleepers during manufacture — no more saw cuts — and you need slightly more than 12V to bridge that gap!

Left: *This shows part of the 20ft by 9ft layout before the basic scenery was built.*

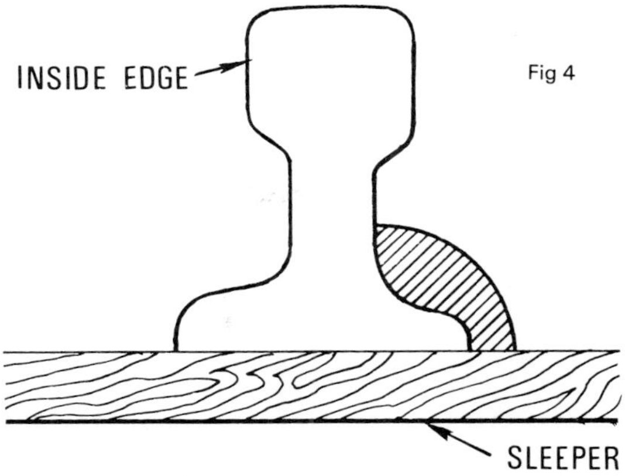

INSIDE EDGE

Fig 4

SLEEPER

After this electrical shock treatment the trackwork was painted black and the top of the rail and the inside edges wiped clean. Cleaning the inside edges of the rail is as important as cleaning the top — fig 4. Model flanges rub along these and therefore increase electrical pick-up chances.

Before the track was relaid, the cork underlay was prepared, by first cutting slots for point tie bars, then drilling suitable holes for the point operating wires, and finally by painting with grey acrylic paint. The track was placed back in its correct final position, again secured with drawing pins and then sprinkled with PSM granite ballast. After the paint had dried excess ballast was removed, the drawing pins taken out and the bare patches so caused were filled.

We do not use this technique now, however. Nowadays, ballast is put into place dry, carefully smoothed off with a small paint brush and correct shoulders built up. Then a 50/50 mixture of Evo-W Resin glue and water, plus a squirt of washing up liquid, is carefully dropped on from a small dropping bottle. This gluey mixture soaks through the ballast and eventually sets, holding everything tight. As far as appearance is concerned this is a far better method, but much more time consuming, ballasting taking longer than track making.

Electrics

For electrification purposes we decided that the layout should be divided into two areas:

a the complete station area and main running lines through the yard.
b the yard itself excluding main running lines.

This decision meant that two control panels had to be built, one for the yard and one for the rest of the layout. In one of the photographs these control panels

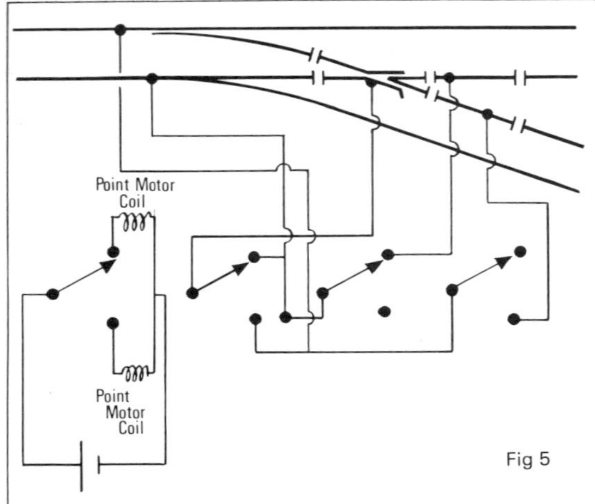

can be seen. The so called signalman sat behind the longer panel and was supposed to conduct the proceedings. The two driver's cabs (cabs as in Cab-Control) can also be seen. In practice, the signalman set up routes, cleared the appropriate signals and then provided power, after which the drivers simply drove their trains. Obviously four people were needed to run a proper show at exhibitions one signalman, one yard operator and two drivers. However actual operating will be discussed later.

Suffice to say that the layout was electrified on the cab-control system having two cabs. The main station was divided into various sections and each section could obtain its power from either cab via a single-pole double-throw centre-off switch. This meant that although nominally Cab A controlled the down line and Cab B the up line, the position could be reversed. This was a very useful facility at exhibitions when we were perhaps running behind time.

Point operation was via H&M point motors, wired up so that the integral switch enabled permanent make contacts to be used as operation switches. In practice however, the point motors were operated through a relay with four changeover contacts. This provided the necessary contacts for wiring up the points themselves — the basic circuitry of which is shown in fig 5.

The point motor power supply was not conventional at all. I should imagine that there are quite a few modellers who have smelt point motor coils cooking and have rushed around trying to find which one is getting hot! Eventually finding the offending coil by following the smoke is little comfort, especially when you know that good money is evaporating as you watch. We had seen this happening a few times, and had quite a number of point motors made up using cannibalised coils. Therefore to overcome this problem of burning out, the 'urge' to throw the motors was provided by a largish capacitor, not from a direct power source. This capacitor was charged by a trickle charger — fig 6. An indicator lamp and a push-for-off

Above left: *Basic point circuitry using relay with 4 change over contacts.*

Right: *A Blue Pullman diesel set passes a coal train just outside Much Bickering station. The siding on the right was built to connect with an industrial tramway which never materialised.*

Below: *Point motor safety device*

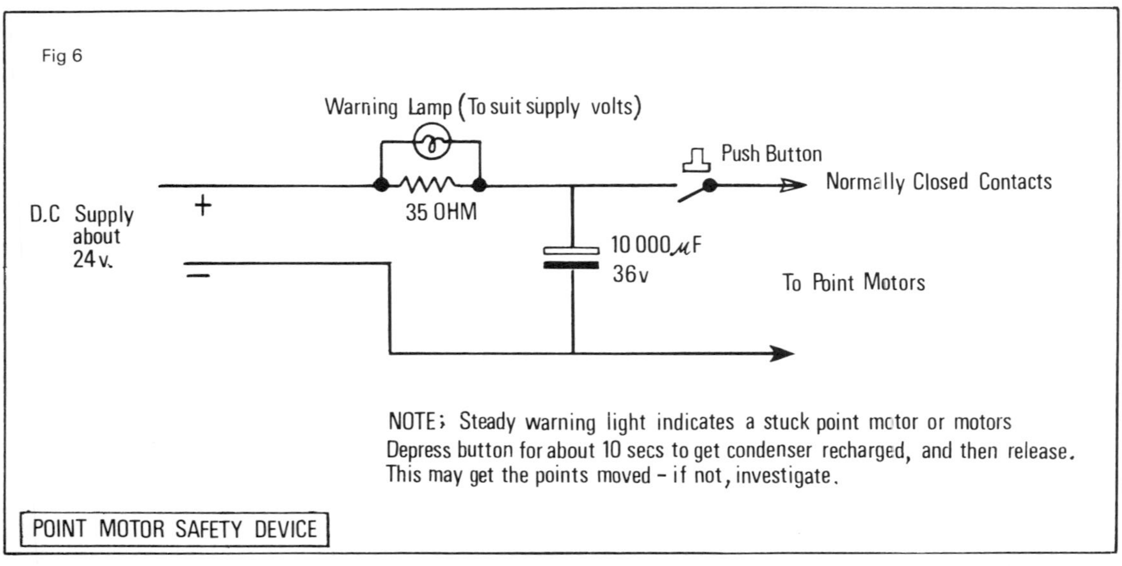

The road side of Much Bickering station with the Post Office the other side of the level crossing.

MUCH BICKERING

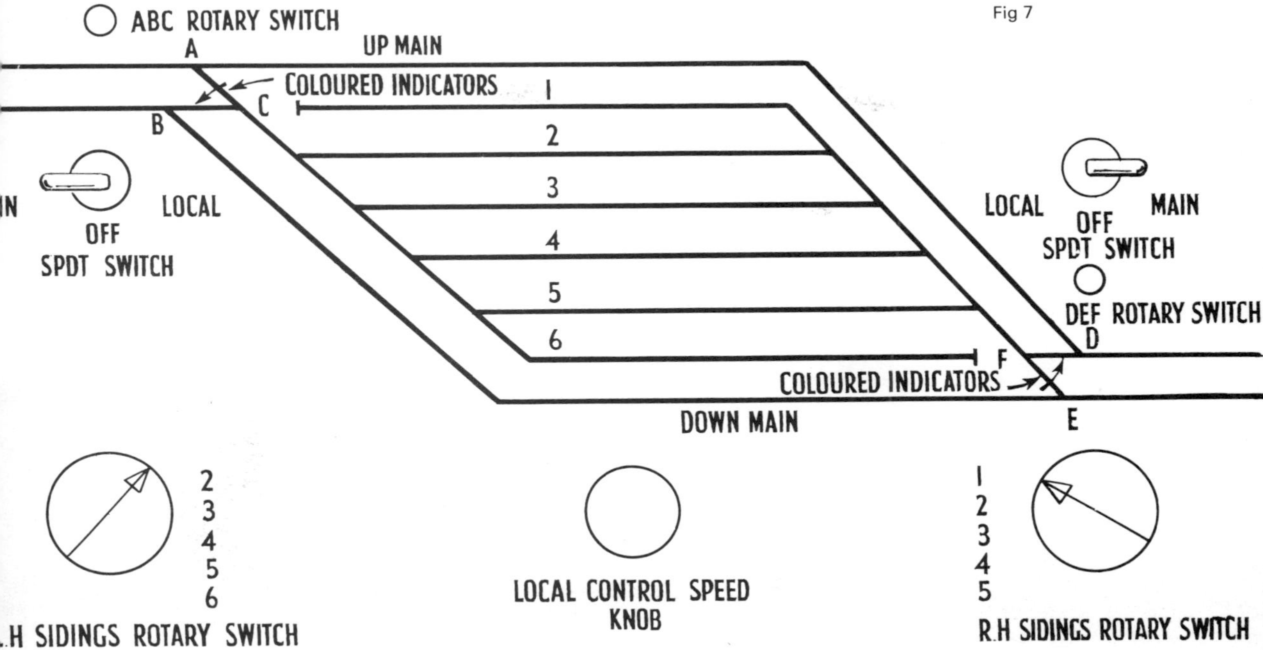

Above: *Local control panel. Sidings 1 and 6 are not open ended. Used for reversible trains e.g. Pullmans, Brighton Belles, DMU etc.*

Left: *An aerial view of Much Bickering station as an Ivatt built 2-6-0 heads a northbound cattle train.*

switch were also in the circuit, and the lamp showed if a point motor had failed to throw fully. If it had, the lamp would light as a trickle current, which would be insufficient to harm the coils, passed through the circuit. Pushing the button would disconnect the capacitor from the motor, it would have a chance to charge up, and on releasing the button there would again be 'urge' available to push the motor across. If nothing 'appened, and the lamp relit, something was wrong with the motor.

After this system was installed no coils burnt out, and we found that the capacitor used had sufficient capacity to power two point motors simultaneously (eg on a cross over) and that in practice there was little to choose — as far as normal performance was concerned — between it and a direct power supply.

This briefly describes the electrical situation on the main panel, but the yard panel had some minor variations, best explained with the aid of a diagram — fig 7.

Yard Control

First, let me point out that the yard controller has no influence over the main running lines, apart from the settings of points ABC and DEF, because power supplies for these lines come from the main panel.

Imagine a train travelling in the Up direction. By moving the point ABC rotary switch to its correct setting, entry to the yard can be effected, the siding entered being determined by the setting of the left hand siding switch. Coloured indicators light up on the mimic diagram of the panel to show the settings of ABC. The power now available in the yard is chosen by throwing the single-pole double-throw centre off power switch which, according to whichever way it is thrown, gives power from the main line, makes it dead, or provides power from the local controller on the yard panel. The same considerations also apply to trains leaving the yard or entering in the Down

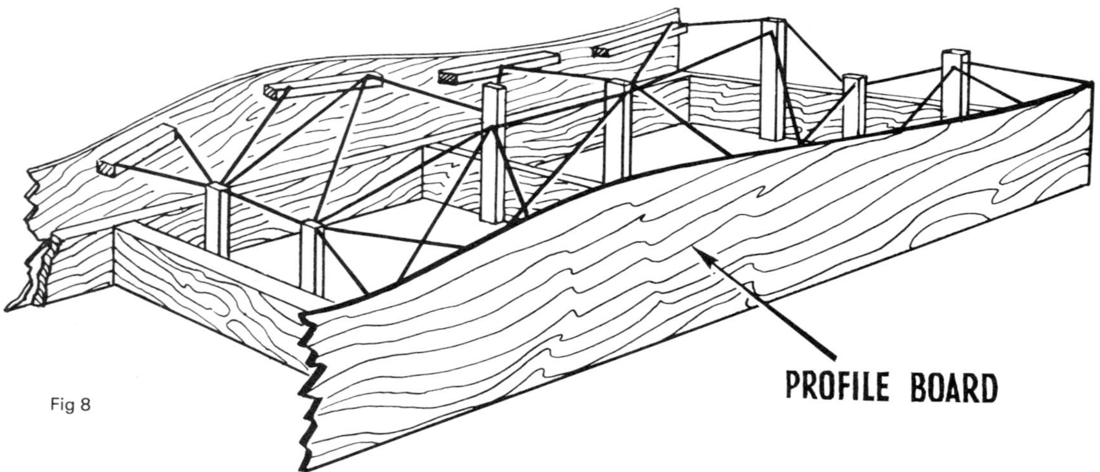

Fig 8

direction. Equally, by the correct setting of the ABC, DEF and left and right hand siding switches through routes can be arranged. All this sounds most complicated, but in practice it is soon picked up and operating the yard panels is quite easy.

It may have dawned on some readers that with siding points under the control of a rotary switch our normal capacitor powered system would soon be drained of power. For example switching from siding 2 to siding 6 would be throwing 5 points in less than 1 second. To overcome this problem, a delay was built into the power circuit, when the power capacitor, if I may use the word, was charged by yet another capacitor. In practice this produced a delay of about 1 second, so that the siding switch could be turned and after a short delay the power would be released. This system worked well, but unfortunately the H&M motors began to be temperamental, and the self switching contacts became unreliable. As a result all were replaced by relays, with wires soldered to the moving armature to act as a gainstroke. These relays also provided the contacts necessary for the power switching at the points. It also meant that complicated protective power supplies were unnecessary so a direct power supply was wired in, and our Capacitor/capacitor system scrapped.

Scenery

Convincing scenery is a most difficult thing to produce in model form, but nevertheless some attempt has to be made. Because the baseboards were becoming rather weighty and cumbersome we decided to use the American Hard shell plaster technique and try a spot of ultra basic 'zip' texturing.

Hard shell plasters require a framework on which they can be built up. This was produced as in fig 8 and as can be seen utilises 1in by 1in (or convenient) risers joined by a web of supporting tape. In our case we used everything from fibre backed self adhesive tape to thick Sellotape. Newspapers were then laid flat and covered by paper towels dipped in a moulding plaster. This paper towelling was repeated twice, until a sufficient thickness had been built up. Then a second type of plaster was put on with a 1½in paint brush. This plaster was peculiar in that when mixed it has the consistency of thin condensed milk, but starts to set immediately it is brushed on. By careful brush work representations of strata may be built up, particularly on vertical faces.

After the plaster has set fully it can be stained with an earth coloured dye, so that if it is chipped the exposed piece does not show through as white.

Earth and grass are both put on in the same way. Firstly powder paints and plaster of paris are mixed together dry (3:1 paint/plaster) to give the required colours. Then the hard shell plaster is sprayed with water from a Celspray, or scent spray, and the earth mixture sprinkled on from a domestic sieve. After all the layout has been earthed it is sprayed with water again and 'grassed' in the same manner. In this way horizontal ledges can be earthed and grassed easily because the scenic material falls vertically and only adheres to the non vertical faces. It can, if done properly, look quite effective.

When this basic scenicing has been done, the overall impression has been completed and detailing can take place. On 'Much Bickering' very few areas received any detailing, the layout was dismantled before we reached that stage.

It is perfectly possible to cut down weight even more, if the layout has to be transported, by removing the supports from beneath the scenery shell. The 1in by 1in risers can be removed and the web of tape taken away. It will be found that the shell is quite strong and is robust enough to take a few hard knocks. If damage does take place, it is easily repaired, a paper towel soaked in plaster slapped over the break, smoothed down and then earthed and grassed.

Buildings

The buildings on Much Bickering are a real hotch potch. The water mill next to the weir is freelance, so is the smaller station building, the weighbridge hut and the very unlikely coal office underneath the buffer stops at the end of the coal staithes. The goods shed is from Effington, and the main station building based on Rotherfield and Mark Cross, drawings of which appeared in the model press a long time ago. I say 'based on' advisedly because if anyone knows this station they will soon realise that certain major liberties have been taken, not only with the arrangement of the buildings but also the finish. Ours is plain brick, the prototype was far different. The signal box is near enough that of the original at Goathland to satisfy us, but under no circumstances could it be called an accurate model. The shops are a mirror image of the set produced by Ken Ball, based on prototypes at Kerridge, and together with the main station building and goods shed are the work of one man.

Left: *Baseboard shown without trackbase. Supports are any convenient pieces of wood.*

Below: *The two control panels.*

The models themselves are not made from Styrene, as is the vogue nowadays, but are made from mounting card, braced with ¼in ramin and stuck with Evo-W-resin glue. The roofs are from 1mm ply and over the years no warping has been noticed.

All in all the station area presents a coherent scene, but is far removed from the original at Goathland.

Other details

Signals are standard Ratio lower quadrants motorised using home made coils. They were first made when the life of the layout was coming to an end and were produced as an experiment to see if our coils would work. Their bases show up rather poorly in the photographs, but on our new layout they will be disguised.

Level crossing gates are stretched Airfix ones and fencing is matchsticks and cotton, except in the station area where it is Airfix again. Nameboards are styrene, Mercontrol tubing, roof finials and paint, and various railway notices are again tubing and painted card.

Operating

Previously I have mentioned that this layout was built to BRMSB scale OO standards, but anyone who has studied them will realise how ridiculous they are and how pointwork could be built to BRMSB standards over which no OO gauge locomotive would run, no matter what its wheel profiles etc. However, it can be shown that a loco with wheel back-to-backs of 14.25mm will still run on Scale track, providing flange thickness and depth is within reasonable limits. What this means in effect is that the old Hornby Dublo, or modern Wrenn locos can be used on scale track. A check on the metal driving wheels of these models reveals a back-to-back of about 14.25mm, and if this dimension is eased to a full 14.25mm by gently tapping the uninsulated axle with a hammer and drift, then they will run. The plastic wheels are a different matter altogether — the moulding process involves shrinkage and goodness knows what — but at least they can be easily and reliably replaced.

All this is leading up to the fact that as far as operating was concerned we relied heavily on proprietary locos and stock with relevant wheels eased or replaced.

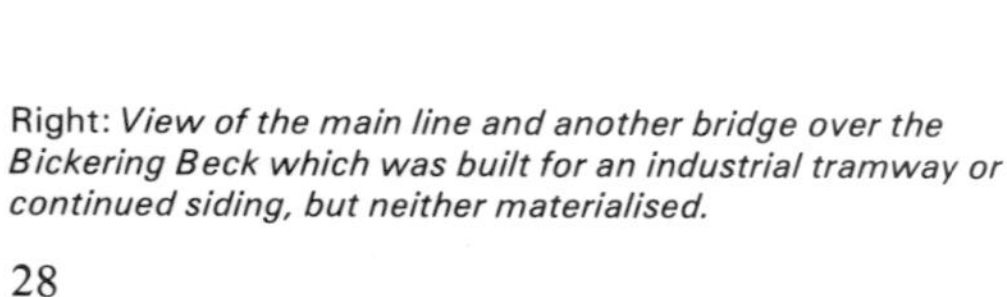

Right: *View of the main line and another bridge over the Bickering Beck which was built for an industrial tramway or continued siding, but neither materialised.*

STATION			YARD	
UP DIRECTION →	← DOWN DIRECTION	TIME	SOUTH END	NORTH END
	D.M.U Dep.Bay	¼		Push-Pull Dep.2
		½	Local Dep. 3	
Push--Pull Arr.Bay		¾		D.M.U Arrival 2
	Local arr. DN.Main	1		
Fig 9	A N D	S O	O N	

The aimless running of some model railways to be seen at exhibitions, with operators shouting, bells clanging and chaos reigning was, we decided, not for us. Far better if we could produce a simple sequence timetable and practice it for months before an exhibition. So, that is what was done. A look at the layout showed that the maximum number of trains which could comfortably be handled was ten. Accordingly ten trains were made up ranging from heavy freight to pick-ups, and express passenger to push-pull units. The whole layout was then drawn out diagrammatically and the names of the trains printed on small pieces of card. They were placed on the diagram in appropriate starting positions and the timetable worked out by moving the cards — so representing train movements. Each move was noted down in the form of instructions for the yard operator and the signalman-fig 9. Each could then tell at a glance what the next train movement was and so set up the appropriate route. Eventually all the pieces of card were made to return to their original starting positions, and hopefully, we had a working timetable, which required no hand shunting.

When we first ran it, the sequence took nearly two hours to complete, but after practice it could be handled in 30 minutes, an ideal time for a show. For exhibition running, a timetable showing train movements in the station was printed and put on display. This had the times of the movements marked and a 30 minute clock was put near at hand. It certainly added interest to the operating and that show (Bristol '71) was probably the most enjoyable the club has ever taken part in — everything working well.

But it must be said that the main reason why it was so enjoyable was the fact that the timetable was well known to us. When four people are needed to run a layout properly they must know exactly what is going on and so pre-show practice is essential. At the time of writing (Feb 75) we are busy practising for the 1975 Bristol exhibition, and we have been doing so since September 74. Needless to say we are not yet perfect.

Future

There is no future for Much Bickering as such. The station area is scrapped and has been replaced by Long Suffren, built for exactly the same reasons as stated at the beginning of the article. Nevertheless, some parts of the layout remain: the storage yards are still in use and the ends still carry traffic but as can be seen from the enclosed track plan of the new layout even these are due for eventual replacement.

Thanks are due to Brian Monaghan for some of the photographs, Mrs J. Adamson who typed the script and finally my personal thanks to all club members, past and present, who helped in any way with the layout, in what was a most enjoyable model railway exercise.

Right: *Another view of Bickering Beck bridge. The handbuilt loco body has a Fleischmann power unit and the wagons are repainted Hornby Dublo products.*

12458
LLANBRADACH

Timetables for all

DAVID J. HYSON
(Member South Western Circle and Gauge O Guild)

I suffer from the unfortunate complaint known as 'Operators Twitch'. I have only to see a model railway layout being operated and my right hand starts to twitch as if I had the controller in my hand. Because of this I have taken the opportunity to operate a wide variety of layouts in various scales and, from this experience I have come to the conculsion that model railway owners are missing a lot if they do not work their layouts to a timetable. For me, a layout without a timetable seems to lack a purpose and its operation lacks the interest it could have. If you would like to have a timetable for your layout but are not sure how to go about preparing one, then I hope that this article may be of use.

Over the years I have constructed many timetables, but for this article I want to draw on my experiences in making timetables for a large layout. In doing this I hope that I can cover the sort of timetabling problems that can arise on any size of layout from the smallest to the largest. Timetabling for a small one man layout is obviously a lot easier than for a large layout, although the basic methods remain the same for any size layout. The layout which I will use as an example was a large O gauge layout, electrically operated, part indoors and part outdoors. It required six or seven operators who had the use of some 40 locomotives plus numerous carriages and wagons. With this sort of layout one meets practically every sort of problem that can arise in timetable construction.

Left: *Much Bickering station photographed before the model was complete, but giving an idea of its appearance as a 2-6-2T approaches with a local train and a slow freight trundles through in the other direction.*

The easiest way to produce a timetable, especially if your layout is modelled on a particular prototype, is to use a copy of the prototype Working Timetable. These contain details of all train movements (except certain light engine movements) but they do not contain locomotive duties, carriage stock rosters, etc. For these you will require the relevant appendices to the working timetables. An example of an L&SWR Working Timetable for the Lyme Regis Branch for the summer of 1909 can be seen at fig 1. The main disadvantages of a Working Timetable are first the long time taken by the prototype to run from one station to another as compared with a model, and second, the long gaps which occur between trains, particularly on branch lines. This introduces us to the problem of time on a model and since this is applicable either when you use a Working Timetable, or when you make your own, we must first decide which sort of time we are going to use.

There are three types of 'time' which can be used when operating model railways. These are sequence, speeded-up time, and real time. Sequence operation is where each movement is allowed to take as long as you like, and each movement, or group of movements is given a sequence number starting from 1. Under operational conditions the operator works through the operations under sequence 1 and then moves on to sequence 2. This method is ideal for the one man layout, but becomes more difficult as the number of operators increases, since no one can move on to the second sequence until everybody has finished the first sequence. Fig 2 shows an operators' instructions for a sequence timetable.

Most model layouts suffer from a scaling down of distance between stations, and to make the time taken for a train to run from one station to the next seem more realistic, many layouts run to a speeded-up clock. By altering the gearing inside a clock it is possible to make the clock go a lot faster — about ten times faster seems to be average. Frankly this alteration to clocks is beyond my capabilities, but there have been articles in the model press from time to time showing how it can be done. There are, however, some disadvantages in this method. If your station layout has similar dimensions to a chosen prototype, then the time taken for shunting, or to run a locomotive round a train will be the same as it takes on the prototype. You will therefore need to allow say, twenty minutes on your timetable for a locomotive to run round its train. The clock will also need some means of stopping it in an emergency, such as a derailment, otherwise you will soon find yourself running several hours late. A final point is that the clock will need to be visible by all operators, or else a slave clock provided for those who cannot see the main one.

Fig 1

LYME REGIS LIGHT RAILWAY.

FOR SPEED RESTRICTIONS SEE PAGES A, B, C & D.

This is a Single Line and is worked under the Regulations for working Single Lines by the Electric Train Tablet Block System.

WEEK DAYS—NO SUNDAY SERVICE.

Distance from Axminster. M.	C.	DOWN TRAINS.	1		2		3		4		5		6		7		8		9		10	
			Pass.				Mixed.		Goods.				Mixed.				*Mixed.*		*Mixed.*			
																	June 1st to July 9th inc. and from Sept. 27th.		*July 10th to Sept. 25th inclusive.*			
			arr.	dep.			arr.	dep.	arr.	dep.			arr.	dep.			arr.	dep.	arr.	dep.		
			a.m.	a.m.			a.m.	a.m.	a.m.	a.m.			p.m.	p.m.			p.m.	p.m.	p.m.	p.m.		
—	—	AXMINSTER	...	8 5	...	...	...	10 37	...	11 50	...	...	...	1 10	...	...	...	3 0	...	3 10	...	...
			After No. 1 Up arrives.				Af. No. 3 or 4 Up arrives.		After No. 5 Up arrives.				After No. 6 Up arrives.				*After No. 8 Up arrives.*		*After No. 8 Up arrives.*			
4	21	Combpyne......	8 17	8 18	...	...	10 49	10 50	12 10	12 13	...	...	1 22	1 23	...	...	3 12	3 13	3 22	3 23	...	...
6	59	LYME REGIS	8 25	...	...	...	10 57	...	12 20	...	...	...	1 30	...	...	...	3 20	...	3 30	...	...	...

DOWN TRAINS.	11		12		13		14		15		16		17		18		19		20	
	Pass.		Mixed.		Mixed.		Mixed.													
	arr.	dep.	arr.	dep.	arr.	dep.	arr.	dep.												
	p.m.	p.m.	p.m.	p.m.	p.m.	p.m.	p.m.	p.m.												
AXMINSTER	...	4 27	...	5 50	...	7 12	...	8 45	...	...	...	...	...	...	...	...	...	...	...	...
	After No. 12 Up arrives.		After No. 13 Up arrives.		After No. 14 Up arrives.		After No. 15 Up arrives.													
Combpyne..................	4 39	4 40	6 2	6 3	7 24	7 25	8 57	8 58	...	...	...	...	...	...	...	...	...	...	...	...
LYME REGIS............	4 47		6 10	...	7 32	...	9 5	...	...	...	...	...	...	...	...	...	...	...	...	...

Distance from Lyme Regis. M.	C.	UP TRAINS.	1		2		3		4		5		6		7		8		9		10	
			Pass.				*Pass.*		*Pass.*		Goods.		Mixed.				Mixed. A					
							Fridays only.		*Not Fridays.*													
			arr.	dep.			arr.	dep.	arr.	dep.	arr.	dep.	arr.	dep.			arr.	dep.				
			a.m.	a.m.			a.m.	a.m.	a.m.	a.m.	a.m.	a.m.	p.m.	p.m.			p.m.	p.m.				
—	—	LYME REGIS	...	7 12	...	...	...	*9 38*	...	*9 48*	...	11 12	...	12 30	...	...	...	2 20	...	...	...	...
							After No. 1 Dn. arrives.		*After No. 1 Down arrives.*		After No. 3 Down arrives.		After No. 4 Dn. arrives.				After No. 6 Down arrives.					
2	38	Combpyne	7 20	7 21	...	...	*9 46*	*9 47*	*9 56*	*9 57*	11 21	11 24	12 38	12 39	...	...	2 28	2 29	...	...	...	...
6	59	AXMINSTER	7 32	...	...	...	*9 58*	...	*10 8*	...	11 36	...	12 50	...	...	...	2 40	...	...	...	...	...

UP TRAINS.	11		12		13		14		15		16		17		18		19		20	
			Pass.		Mixed.		Mixed.		Mixed.											
			arr.	dep.	arr.	dep.	arr.	dep.	arr.	dep.										
			p.m.	p.m.	p.m.	p.m.	p.m.	p.m.	p.m.	p.m.										
LYME REGIS	...	...	...	3 55	...	4 55	...	6 30	...	8 15	...	...	...	...	...	...	...	...	...	...
			After Nos. 8 or 9 Dwn. arrs.		After No. 11 Down arrives.		After No. 12 Down arrives.		After No. 13 Down arrives.											
Combpyne......	...	...	4 3	4 4	5 3	5 4	6 38	6 39	8 23	8 24	...	...	...	...	...	...	...	...	...	...
AXMINSTER	...	...	4 15	...	5 15	...	6 50	...	8 35	...	...	...	...	...	...	...	...	...	...	...

A Vac. Road Box Lyme Regis to Nine Elms by this Train.

The load of Passenger and Mixed Trains must not exceed 40 wheels.

The load of Down Goods Trains may be made up to 48 wheels when not more than 6 loads of coal or equally heavy minerals. The load of Up Goods Trains may be 60 wheels when it consists principally of empty wagons.

Fig 2

SEQUENCE TIMETABLE

Sweet Hallow Valley Station

Seq. No	*Operation to be carried out*
1	Locomotive from Engine Shed to Goods Yard. Collect two milk tankers and attach these to the train standing in Platform 1. Return Locomotive to Engine Shed.
2	Express Locomotive from Engine Shed to train in Platform 1.
3	Shunting Locomotive from Engine Shed to train standing in Goods Arrival road.
4	Express train departs from Platform 1 to Badgers Beach
5	Locomotive shunts train from Goods Arrival road to Platform 1
6	Passenger train arrives at Platform 2 from Badgers Beach. Train locomotive proceeds to Engine Shed
7	Passenger Train departs from Platform 1 to Badgers Beach
8	Passenger train arrives at Platform 1 from Badgers Beach

From these comments you will no doubt be aware that my preference is for using real time, even if it means that the time taken for a train to run from one station to another is as short as ½ minute. On a large layout all operators can synchronise their watches so that there is no need for a master clock. In compiling a timetable using real time it should not be necessary to use a smaller division of time than ½ minute, since by the time an operator has read his instructions and set the points and signals, at least ½min will have passed. The instructions that I will be giving when it comes to constructing a timetable will apply to real time, but of course, it is no problem to substitute speeded-up time should you so desire.

Having decided what form of time we are going to use, we can now consider some other small problems which we really ought to sort out before we actually start work on the timetable. Every layout has its 'timetable limiter'. This may be an operator, a station, a junction, or even a piece of single track between two stations. What do I mean by a 'limiter'? Well, you may have a friend who regularly comes to help you operate your layout. He has a preference for operating a particular station. Now if he is what I would call a slow operator, it is no good giving him too many trains to deal with in the timetable, since he will only get hopelessly behind. On the other hand it is far more likely that your timetable limiter is a particular station or junction. There is a physical limit to the number of trains that can be worked through this particular stretch of track in a given time. The Southern Region have a notorious 'timetable limiter' in Borough Market Junction, which virtually decides the pattern of BR services in South-East England. On our layout the limiter was Badgers Beach. This had to feed traffic through from two terminii on either side, one terminus being reached via a flat junction with the main line and a long stretch of single track. In addition it had to cope with terminating suburban services and Goods trains. The whole timetable had to be designed to get as many trains as possible through this station without making impossible demands on the station operators.

You will also need to know the number of coaches which can be stored on each coach siding, and the maximum number of goods wagons which can be accommodated on each goods arrival road. If certain lines or sidings are prohibited to certain locos then you must ensure that these are not timetabled to traverse them. You will also need to know the maximum hauling capacity of each loco over the steepest gradient on your line. Each loco can then be put into a haulage class. This can be similar to the old British Railways code running from 8P and 9F for the strongest passenger and goods engine right down to 0P and 0F for the smallest engines. For example you could decide that any 8P engine must be capable of starting from a standing position a 9 coach train on the steepest grade on your line. Then any train which comprises 9 coaches will require an 8P engine to haul it. As an example fig 3 shows the haulage class for some of the locomotives on our layout. You will also

Fig 3

SWEET HALLOW VALLEY RAILWAY
LOCOMOTIVE HAULAGE CAPACITIES

Engine	*Maximum haulage Coaches*	*Capacity Wagons*	*Power Classification*
GWR 2-4-2T	5	18	5P 6F
GWR 0-6-0T	7	24	7P 8F
GWR 0-6-0	4	14	4P 5F
GWR 4-6-0	8	28	8P
SVR 0-6-2T	7	24	7P 8F
LMS 4-6-2	7	24	7P
LNE 2-8-2	8	28	8P
GNR 2-8-0	6	21	7F
LNW 4-6-0 etc., etc.			

need to make a timing list for the routine operatrions at each station; for example, the time taken for a locomotive to run round its train, or to be turned on the turntable, and so on. One important requirement will be to know the time taken by each sort of train between stations. This can be worked out either by running trains at correct speeds between stations and timing them, or by measuring the distance between stations, converting that distance then into scale miles. Knowing the average speed for different types of train it is possible to work out the actual time that should be taken. As an example, in 4mm scale, 67ft (approx) on our model represents one mile on the prototype; therefore if we have an actual distance of 22⅓ft between two stations the prototype distance is ⅓mile. An express running non-stop at 90mph would take 13 seconds to travel between these two stations, whereas a stopping passenger train running at a start to stop average of 30mph would take 40 sec. For the mathematically minded this could be an interesting exercise, but those, like myself, who are not endowed with a bright mathematical mind will probably prefer the easier task of physically timing their trains between stations.

If you wish to run a particular pattern of services on your line then it would be as well to jot this down at this stage so that you have a continual reminder of the pattern of services you are trying to create as you make your timetable. If you refer to fig 4, which shows a simplified block diagram of our layout, you will be able to follow the type of services we try to work. The basic service was an LMSR or LNER express service from Deepwood to Scotland calling at Viaduct Junction to change locomotives. (Viaduct Junction represented Carlisle). A stopping passenger service worked from Deepwood to Viaduct Junction, connecting there with another service to Scotland. A frequent electric multiple unit service worked from Deepwood (Works Platform) to the Push-Pull Terminus just past Badgers Beach station. Heather Hill was the terminus for the GWR trains which worked both express and stopping services to Sweet Hallow Valley. The stopping service usually connected with a Badgers Beach to Viaduct Junction stopping service at Badgers Beach. We also had to fit in stopping goods trains calling at all stations, as well as fitted express goods and parcel trains. The line was mainly double track although the section from Deepwood to Heather Hill and from Badgers Beach to Sweet Hallow Valley was single. Locomotives from trains arriving at Heather Hill had to proceed light to Deepwood as there were no turning facilities at Heather Hill. As our operating session was a weeknight evening, and we needed at least ½ hour to clean the track and get the stock out beforehand, we found that a two hour operating session was about right. Each timetable therefore aimed to get all locomotives and carriages (but not goods wagons) back to their originating point at the end of the session.

It was my main aim to keep each operator fully occupied as far as possible since I have long since learnt that an idle operator can be a menace. He very often starts talking to another operator, who is probably working flat out to get a train ready. He gets delayed by the talking, and so his train is late away, causing problems for another operator — hence my aim 'keep them all busy'. All stations, except Viaduct Junction were normally single manned, although if we had a spare operator, we would put them on Badgers Beach to prevent delays there.

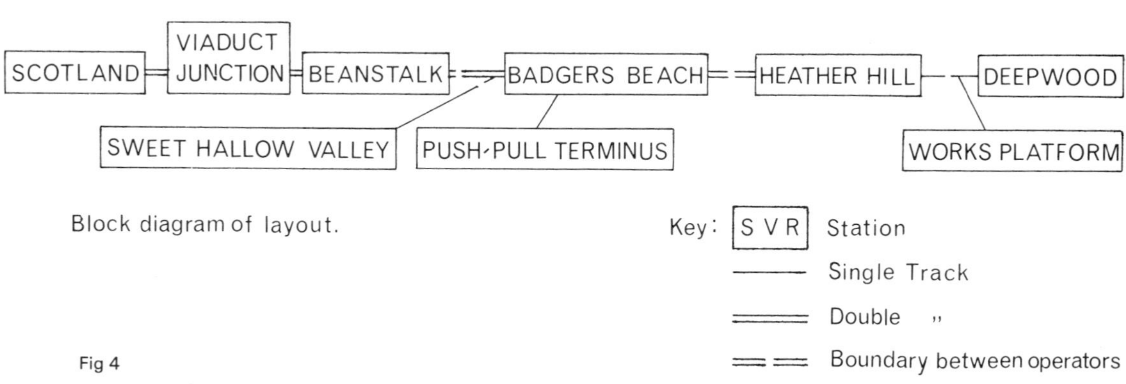

Block diagram of layout.

Fig 4

Armed with all these objectives and information it is possible to start work on the timetable. For a first attempt I would recommend spending a whole evening on the first stage, which is plotting the graph — it is much easier if you can complete the graph at one sitting, and it will probably take you a whole evening to do this at your first attempt. You will need a sheet of graph paper, if possible a transparent ruler or set square (better than a boxwood one as they won't obscure the graph), a soft pencil and rubber. On the graph paper plot time in the x or horizontal direction (½ min per small graph square). The stations are marked vertically with one graph line allowed for each platform, another for the goods arrival Road, one for each carriage siding and one for the loco shed (with a small layout you could if you like allow a line for each siding). Have a vertical distance of about ½in to 1in between the bottom line used for one station and the top one used for the next. Enter both station names, platform numbers and the times in ink, to prevent subsequent erasure when you have to rub out graph lines. There is no reason, of course, why you should not plot your times up the side of the graph paper and the station names across the paper.

If you have visitors who come to watch your layout in operation, then it is a good idea to get a train moving as soon as possible. On our layout we have the electric multiple unit which is normally stored at the works platform at Deepwood. Being a self contained unit we can start it moving as soon as the timetable starts. Accordingly we mark a dot on the graph at the intersection of the vertical line 0.0 min and the horizontal line representing the works platform at Deepwood. (See fig 5). We know that it takes one minute for a slow train to run from Deepwood to Heather Hill and that trains from Deepwood normally call at platform 2 at Heather Hill, so we can put another pencil dot at the intersection of the 1.0 min vertical line and the Heather Hill platform 2 horizontal line. Joining these two dots up we get the first line on the graph (shown as a solid line marked 1 on fig 5), and this shows the progress of the train from Deepwood to Heather Hill. At Heather Hill the train stands for ½ min in platform 2 and this is shown by a horizontal line one division long. The train now takes ½ min to run to Badgers Beach, and here, since it terminates at the Push Pull Terminus, it must use platform 3. So with a pencil dot at the intersection of the 2.0 min and Badgers Beach platform 3 lines, we now draw another line showing the train movement between Heather Hill and Badgers Beach. After ½ min stand at Platform 3, again shown with a horizontal line, the train takes another ½ min to reach the Push Pull terminus, where it terminates. So another dot at the 3.0 min and Push Pull Terminus intersection is joined by a short line to the 2.0½ departure from Badgers Beach to complete the train's journey. At this stage draw a short length of horizontal pencil line along the Push Pull Terminus line to remind you that it is occupied by a train, and that you will later need to provide a return working. It is also advisable to write beside the graph line the locomotive and stock used on the train. This should be done in pencil and will be used to help compile the operators instructions later on and can then be erased.

Having completed the first train we can now consider another. Once again we will start from Deepwood, although you could of course start from any station. The first train will be at Heather Hill 1 min after the start of the timetable so we can now consider another train commencing at 1.0 min. This time we are going to run an express, so the first stage is for a light engine to go from the engine shed to the carriage siding. Now I would suggest that on your final graph you show light engine movements in a different colour from passenger trains, which should again be in a different colour from freight trains. This principle has been adopted for the finished timetable (fig 6), but on fig 5 I have shown each train in a different symbol, so that you can see better the particular train with which we are dealing. The train which we are now forming is shown with a peck and a dot and with a crossbar on each peck. It is also numbered 2 on the graph. From fig 5 you can see that the light engine goes from the engine shed to the carriage sidings at 1.0min couples up to the empty coaching stock, (our carriages are kept in sets) and departs from the carriage sidings to platform 2 at 2.0½ min. The locomotive is now at the buffer stops and we require an engine for the train. This leaves the engine shed at 4.0½ min and couples to the train. The express departs at 6.0½ min and runs directly to platform 2 at Viaduct Junction. If you refer to fig 4 you will see that trains running between Deepwood and Viaduct Junction do not pass along the line between Badgers Beach and Sweet Hallow Valley, and a gap is therefore left in the train line on the graph over this section. Following our previous pattern we leave a line horizontally along platform 2 at Viaduct Junction to remind us that we have a train here. We will also have to leave a line along platform 2 at Deepwood as we still have the loco which brought the train in, standing at the buffer-stops, and we will have to dispose of this later.

This has kept the operator at Deepwood busy for the first 7 minutes, but what about the other operators? Sweet Hallow Valley has no train yet and Viaduct Junction's first train is the arrival of the express at 9.0 min. So let us put on a stopping train from Viaduct Junction to Deepwood. This is train number 3 on the graph, shown with short pecked lines. Being a local train we can use the loco for the train to

DEEPWOOD
PLATFORM 1
" 2
" 3
WORKS PLATFORM
GOODS ARRIVAL
ENGINE SHED
CARRIAGE SIDING

HEATHER HILL
PLATFORM 1
" 2
" 3
GOODS ARRIVAL

BADGERS B'CH
PLATFORM 1
" 2
" 3
GOODS ARRIVAL
LOCO. SIDING
PUSH – PULL TERM'S

SW'T HALLOW Vy.
PLATFORM 1
" 2
" 3
GOODS ARRIVAL
ENGINE SHED

BEANSTALK
PLATFORM 1
" 2

VIADUCT JC.
PLATFORM 1
" 2
" 3
" 4
GOODS ARRIVAL
ENGINE SHED
CARRIAGE SIDING

LOOP 1
2
3
4

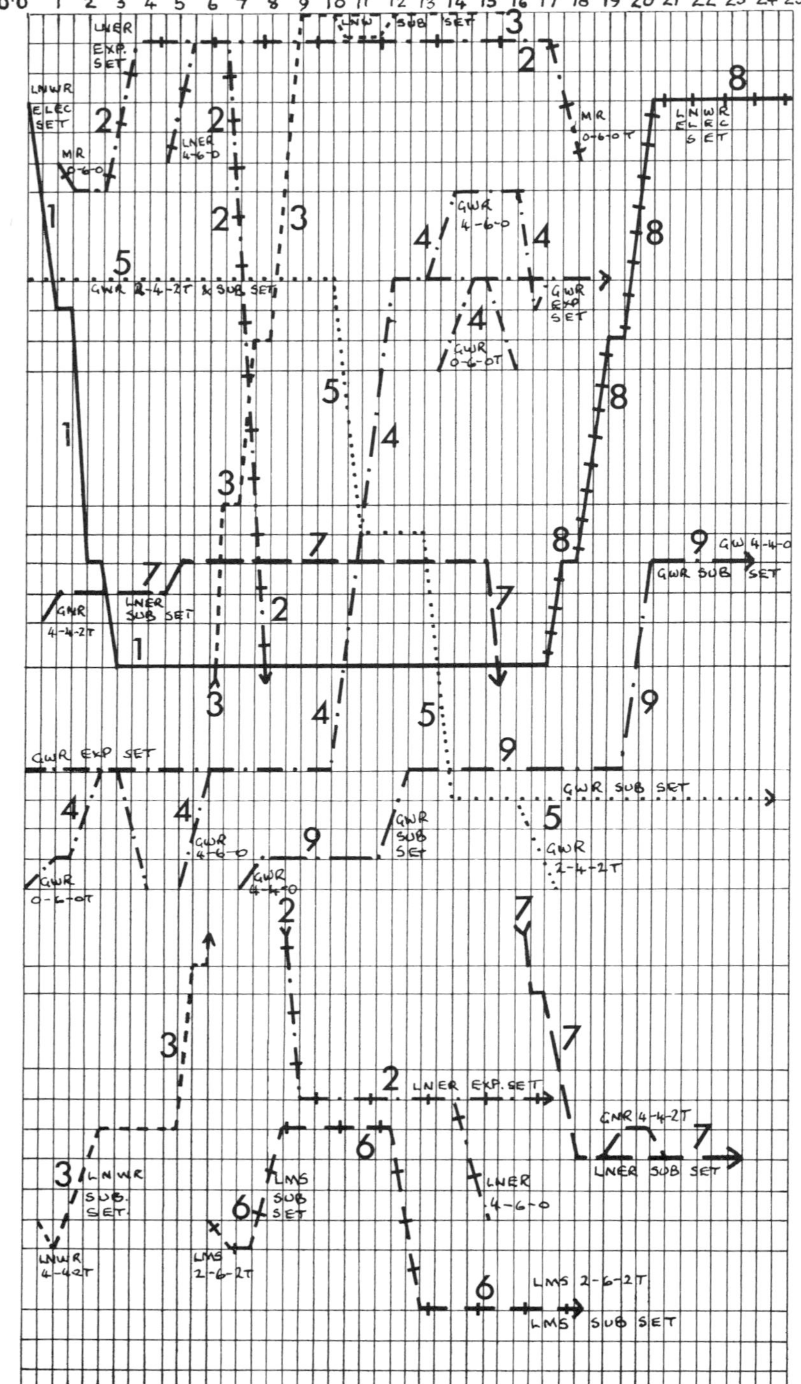

Fig 5

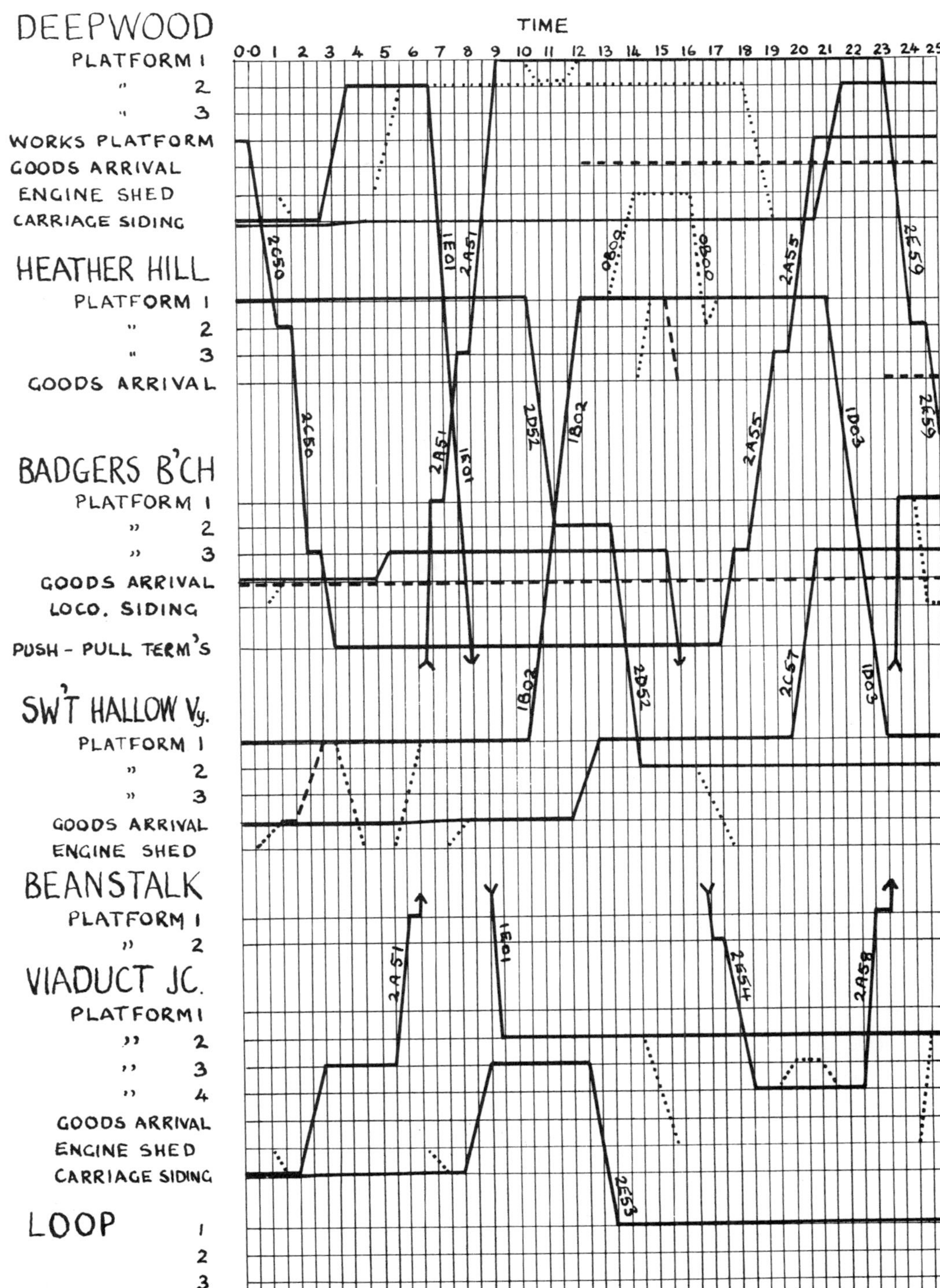

Fig 6

collect it's own stock from the carriage sidings, which it places in platform 3 at 2.0½ min. Allowing the passengers a minute to board we could send it off at 3.0½ min. However this would mean that it would be traversing the single track section between Deepwood and Heather Hill at the same time as the express train which we have just plotted. We do not want it to depart from Heather Hill until 8.0 min, so in this case we plot the path of the train backwards from Heather Hill, allowing our standard ½ min stop at each station. This gives us a Viaduct Junction departure time of 5.0 min. Trains 2 and 3 now pass each other between Heather Hill and Badgers Beach which is double track. (Note that there must be no lines crossing each other on the graph along single track sections, in our case between Deepwood and Heather Hill and Badgers Beach and Sweet Hallow Valley.) Train 3 now arrives at Deepwood at 9.0 min. Local trains normally use platform 1 at Deepwood since, as the locomotives do not require to visit the shed between trips, they can use the run round loop via platform 2 to reach the other end of their train. This run round move commences at 10.0 min. Note that we still have a locomotive in platform 2, but this is at the buffer stops clear of the crossover and is on an electrical section which can be switched out to allow the run round to take place.

We noted earlier that Sweet Hallow Valley has no train as yet and also that Heather Hill has not been particularly busy, so we can alter this by running a GWR express from Sweet Hallow Valley to Heather Hill (Train 4 on the graph, shown by a long peck and dot). Since this is the first train of the day from the country to the town, it can be used to convey milk tankers. To attach these to the coaches berthed in platform 1 (by virtue of there being no carriage siding at Sweet Hallow Valley), the station pilot proceeds to the goods yard, picks up the tankers and places them on the rear of the train. The loco returns to the shed and the express loco runs from the shed to couple up to the train. It was only after a trial run of the timetable (dealt with later) that we found that the time allocated to these moves was inadequate since the milk tankers had to be shunted out from the mixture of wagons in the goods yard. As a result the express ran late. Accordingly we delayed departure until 10.0 min (the time shown on fig 5). Upon arrival at the terminal platform (1) at Heather Hill, the express loco requires to be turned. Since there is no turntable at Heather Hill it proceeds light to Deepwood for turning, running back through Heather Hill Station via platform 2 and then reversing back on to its train in platform 1. Now it could be argued that an express loco will require longer for servicing at an engine shed than allowed in our timetable, but we justify the action by saying that the run from Sweet Hallow Valley to Heather Hill is only a medium distance and that all major servicing can take place at Sweet Hallow Valley. (In practise, Deepwood shed is always too full of stock without providing storage for locos from Heather Hill). Note that while the locomotive is being turned at Deepwood, the Heather Hill Station Pilot removes the milk tankers to the yard. It is now, perhaps, a convenient time to consider a return working from Heather Hill to Sweet Hallow Valley. We have a Suburban train set, which is normally stored between operating sessions in platform 1 at Heather Hill. Clearly this set will need to be moved from platform 1 before the arrival of the express. Because we have no loco facilities at Heather Hill the train engine is normally stored with its train in platform 1, hence we have a train already to go. However Sweet Hallow Valley will be fully occupied until the departure of the express, and in turn Heather Hill will want to have at least a minute after the departure of the slow train to reset the road ready for the arrival of the Express. By looking at the train graph thus far we can see that Heather Hill will be finished with the up local (train 3) by 9.0 min, so that he would have time to set up the road and send off the local to Badgers Beach at 10.0 min. (This is train 5 shown in dots on fig 5). Notice here the interesting sort of situation that can develop at stations. If Deepwood is late sending the express off at 6.0½ then Heather Hill must be late in sending the local (train 3) down to Deepwood because of the single track between Deepwood and Heather Hill. This will probably mean (since most operators seem to work through their operating instructions in sequence) that he will be late in sending the local off to Sweet Hallow Valley. Before he has had a chance to ask Badgers Beach for 'section clear' for the local train, he is offered the express from Badgers Beach. What should he do?, bring the express to a stand outside the station to wait for the local to leave platform 1 or run the express into platform 3 and hope for time to shunt it in to platform 1 later? Whatever he does, it makes operating interesting for him.

Meanwhile our local train (train 5) has reached platform 2 at Badgers Beach. Here it should connect with a train to Viaduct Junction, so we must see to it that the Viaduct Junction train is standing at platform 3 ready to receive the passengers and parcels from Heather Hill. The plotting of the Viaduct Junction train can wait for a moment, but instead of allowing our train to Sweet Hallow Valley the usual ½ min stop at Badgers Beach, we will allow the train 2 min before proceeding to Sweet Hallow Valley where it terminates at platform 2 at 0.14. Having reached the terminus we can leave the coaches in the platform ready for the return journey and send the locomotive to the shed.

In the meantime things have been rather quiet at Viaduct Junction. We have an express which arrives at

9.0, the stock of which we will require later for a return express to Deepwood, so it would be a good idea to provide a connecting train to Scotland for the passengers who arrived on the express. Scotland is, of course represented by the return loop. We therefore send a loco to the carriage siding to pick up a set of coaches (train 6 shown as a pecked line with cross bars) and to proceed to platform 3 at 7.0½ ready for the arrival of the express from Deepwood. After allowing passengers time to change trains the local can leave at 12.0 min and proceed to the loop, where, since it is the first arrival it can occupy the front section of the loop ready to re-appear, after a decent interval, as a train from Scotland.

We mentioned earlier about a connecting train from Badgers Beach to Viaduct Junction connecting with the 10.0 departure from Heather Hill. As you can already see from the graph, the operator at Badgers Beach is getting quite busy, so we will have to fit in the movements whenever we can. The locomotive (train 7 shown as long pecks) could proceed from the locomotive siding to the goods arrival, where the coaches are stored, at the start of the timetable. Having stored the emu at 3.0 we can then draw the coaches into platform 3. It can remain here until it is time for it to depart. It will need to leave as soon after train 4's departure to Sweet Hallow Valley as possible. However the operator at Viaduct Junction is busy until 15.0 min, so we will have to wait until then to move the train off. Once away it proceeds to platform 4 at Viaduct Junctions calling, as do all local trains, at Beanstalk on the way. Upon arrival at Viaduct Junction the locomotive runs round its train ready to form the return working.

It is now time to return to our first train, the emu standing in the Push Pull Terminus at Badgers Beach. We can start a return working (train 8 shown as a solid line with cross ticks) from the terminus at 17.0, and, allowing all the normal stops arrive at Deepwood Works Platform at 20.0½ min.

At this stage it is advisable to look along the graph to see which operator has long periods of inactivity. Heather Hill is quiet from 2.0 to 7.0 min and Sweet Hallow Valley is not at all busy. We could therefore fit in a Suburban Train from Sweet Hallow Valley to Badgers Beach and Heather Hill. We could use the stock of the train arriving at 0.14, but as we have plenty of coaches we decide to use another set. This I have marked as train 9 shown with a long peck and dot. The locomotive has time to go from the engine shed to the coaches stored in the goods arrival before the departure of the express at 10.0 and after this can then draw the coaches into platform 1. The actual arrival at Badgers Beach will be after they have dealt with Train 8 so that the departure from Sweet Hallow Valley will be at 19.0½. We can leave the train for the moment at Badgers Beach as we will probably want to connect with a train from Viaduct Junction. This just leaves us Heather Hill whose spare moments can be occupied in preparing a freight train.

Well, the timetable graph is beginning to take shape, and I hope that you have been able to follow the way in which I prepare my timetable graphs and so be able to make your own. The finished graph is shown in fig 6 and is different insofar as we have redrawn the graph lines with a different code — solid lines for passenger trains, pecked lines for goods and dots for light engines. We have also given each train a reporting number, using in this case the British Rail four letter code. For those unfamiliar with this code, the first number indicates the train type — 1 Express, 2 Suburban, 3-8 Various types of Goods Train, 9 Local unfitted goods, 0 Light Engine. The second letter indicates the destination of the train, in our case A = Deepwood, B = Heather Hill, C = Push Pull Terminus, D= Sweet Hallow Valley and E = Viaduct Junction and Scotland. The last two numbers indicate the train reporting number. On our layout it was 01 upwards for goods and express passenger trains, 50 upwards for local passenger trains and 00 for light engines. It is useful to give each train a reporting number and to print it in the Operator's instructions, especially if it is a large layout, as it makes train tracing on the graph much easier.

While you are adding the train reporting numbers, make a separate list giving the train reporting number, departure time, train route and Locomotive and stock used, as for example: 2V56 3.15 Waterloo-Exeter. Warship Diesel, 8 Coach Buffet Set 215.

On completion of this table, the information on train formation originally pencilled on the graph can be rubbed off. We have done this, as you can see, on fig 6. The train list can be used later to prepare loco workings and also carriage workings, should you wish to go into such detail. On our layout goods trains are shown in this list with a loco and guards van plus a note as to the maximum permissible length of the train. You may however prefer to provide a complete list of the wagons and vans to be conveyed by each train.

If you are making a graph for the first time it is a good idea to have a sketch diagram of your layout on which is marked the length of each platform and siding. This need only be a very rough diagram. Make small slips of paper for each locomotive and carriage, or sets of carriages. On the slip of paper write the locomotive or coach number and its overall length. This procedure can also be used for goods wagons if your layout is small, but for large layouts there are other systems which are described later. At the commencement of the graph put your pieces of paper on the correct position of the diagram and as you plot each movement on the graph move the pieces of paper

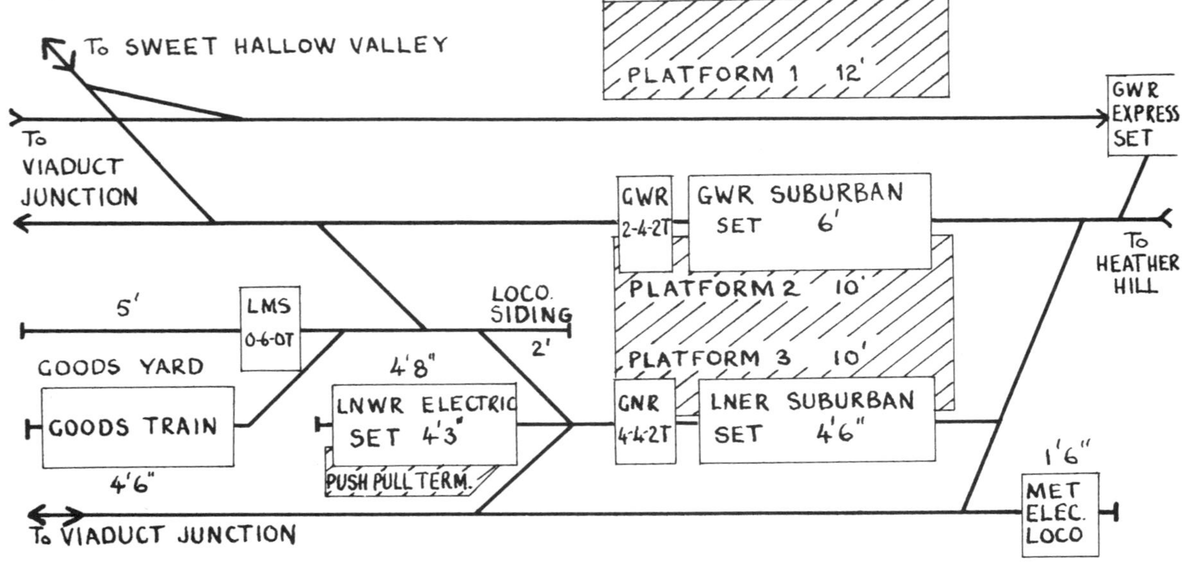

Fig 8

BRITISH RAILWAYS CARRIAGE STOCK ROSTA FOR WATERLOO

Time	*Destination*	*Formation*	*Platform*	*Train formed from previous service:-*		
				Time	*From*	*Due*
11.30R	Bournemouth West	1 S.K. 1 B.S.K. 1 C.K. 1 R.K.B. 1 R.C.O 1 S.O. 1 B.S.K. 3 set(k)	10	10.57	Clapham Yd	11.06
11.40	Clapham Jc (Kensington Sidings)	Vans, etc. 1 B.Y.	Dock	—	Waterloo to provide	—

BRITISH RAILWAYS LOCOMOTIVE DUTY FOR WILLESDEN

Duty No 45	Class 4 (Ex L.M.S. 2-6-0)	
	arr (a.m.)	Dep (a.m.)
Watford M.P.D.		8.57 L.E.
Hemel Hempstead	9.20	9.53
Berkhampstead	10.07	10.22 Attach any North Traffic
Tring	10.35	
	Shunt	
Tring		2.40 p.m.
Berkhampstead	2.52p.m.	3.33
Hemel Hempstead	3.43	4.10
Watford Junction	4.35	4.40 L.E. to Watford M.P.D.

representing the engine and stock to the position shown on the graph, making certain that the platforms and sidings are long enough to accommodate the train. Fig 7 shows such a diagram of Badgers Beach Station at 11.0 min. This clearly shows the GWR express moving off to the right, and the fact that platform 1 is the only vacant platform. If you have a small one man layout you can, of course, do the same thing by just moving your stock as you plot each move on the graph. However if you have a large layout with several operators, then the better method is to use the slips of paper. Using either of these methods you will not forget the existence of trains on certain parts of the layout, which can happen if you only draw the graph.

You will notice from our graph that, as yet, no goods trains have moved. This is due to the fact that the methods of goods train operation on our line require a great deal of shunting before they are ready to depart.

Now is the best time, if you require it, to make your locomotive and rolling stock rostas. If you are a perfectionist, this list will show up too short loco turnround times, inadequate utilisation of stock and so on. I have never provided these sort of lists for our layout because we have always had a superabundance of locos and stock. However for those with more modest means it is a good idea to allocate locomotives and stock for each train. If you do not operate your coaches in sets you will also need to give exact instructions for which coaches are to go into which train. To give you an idea of how the finished stock rosta should look, fig 8 shows a typical British Rail example.

We have now reached the stage where we can begin to compile the operator's instructions for each station. The amount of detail you incorporate is obviously dependant on your own needs and that of your operators. For example you may need to give details of which section switches need to be switched on and which signal and point levers need to be pulled for each movement. This was not necessary on our layout as fig 9 which shows part of the operators instructions for Deepwood. The train reporting number is included firstly, so that in the event of any problems the operator can refer to the train number when reporting the problem to the controller and secondly, so that the operator knows which Bell Code to use when passing the train to the next operator.

Each operator, especially if your layout is an outdoor one, or portable, will also need a list giving the position of each locomotive and item of rolling stock at the commencement of the timetable. The operating instructions need to be protected from wear in some way. This can be done either by writing instructions on cards, or by protecting the instructions behind some form of transparent plastic. The cheapest method is to

Fig 9

SWEET HALLOW VALLEY RAILWAY

DEEPWOOD OPERATORS INSTRUCTIONS.

Position of Locomotives and stock at commencement of Timetable.

Works Platform: LNWR Electric Multiple Unit
Carriage Siding 1: LMS Express set
Carriage Siding 2: LMS Suburan set
Engine Shed: LMS 0-6-0T, LMS 4-6-2, and others.

Time	*Operation*	*Train No*
0.00	Train from Works Platform to Heather Hill	2C50
0.01	LMS 0-6-0T from Engine Shed to train in Carriage Siding 1.	
0.02½	Train from Carriage Siding 1 to Platform 2	
0.04½	LMS 4-6-2 from Engine Shed to train in Platform 2	
0.06½	Express departs from Platform 2 to Heather Hill	1E01
0.09	Suburban train arrives at Platform 1 from Heather Hill	2A51
0.10	Loco runs round train in Platform 1	
0.12	Commence to prepare Goods Train for Badgers Beach ready to depart at 0.59	
0.14	Light engine arrives at Engine Shed from Heather Hill for turning	0B00
0.16	GWR engine departs from Engine Shed to Heather Hill	0B00
0.18	Light Engine from Platform 2 to train in Carriage Siding 2	
0.20½	Train arrives at Works Platform from Heather Hill	2A55
0.21	Train from Carriage Siding 2 to Platform 2	
0.23	Suburban Train departs from Platform 1 to Heather Hill	2E59

and so on until 2.00

mount the instructions on corrugated cardboard and put this inside a plastic bag which is selotaped into a tight skin covering the instructions.

The graph method may not seem to have much relevance to the person who has a circular layout. However if, instead of platforms and sidings we insert electrical section numbers, we can still construct our graph. It is probable that the circle of track will come under one section, and that the time will be known for a train to make one circuit of the track. The planning line on the graph will then stay in one electrical section for an amount of time equal to the number of circuits of the circle required before moving on to another section. Fig 10 shows a simple layout and the start of a timetable graph next to it. Just to show you that you do not have to have the time going across the graph,

Below: *Timetable graph for circular layout shown on right half of diagram.*

Fig 10

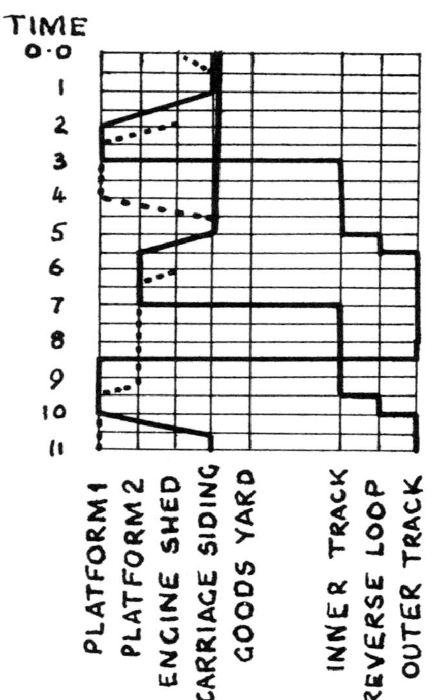

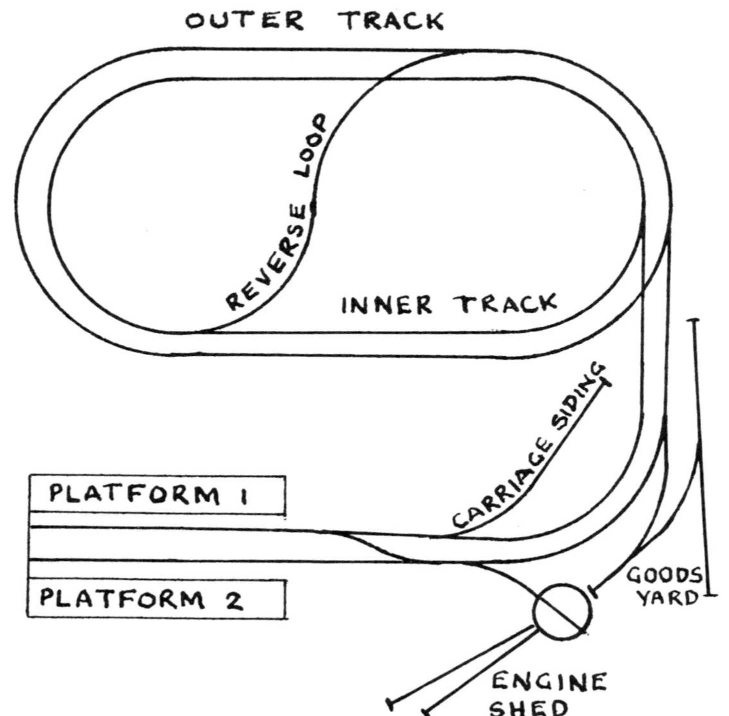

Fig 11

WAGON ATTACH AND DETACH INSTRUCTIONS FOR DEEPWOOD

First Goods Train

DETACH DETACH ATTACH DETACH DETACH ATTACH
DETACH DETACH DETACH DETACH ATTACH ATTACH
ATTACH DETACH ATTACH ATTACH DETACH ATTACH

Second Goods Train

ATTACH ATTACH DETACH DETACH ATTACH DETACH
DETACH ATTACH ATTACH DETACH ATTACH DETACH
etc, etc.

we have made it going down the side. In this case a light engine goes from the engine shed to the carriage siding at 0.0, collects the coaches and places them in platform 1. Another engine leaves the shed at 0.2, couples up to the train and departs at 0.3. It circuits the inner track until 0.5 when it crosses via the reverse loop and circuits the outer track until 8.0½ when it returns to platform 1. You will no doubt be able to work out the other moves from the graph. This method of graph construction may also be favoured by the person whose line consists of long stretches of single track, since he will principally be concerned with the length of time that a train occupies the single track sections.

At this stage I would recommend having a run using the timetable. You will have to run goods trains at this stage as block trains without any shunting at stations as we will be considering goods train make up later on. It is suprising how many mistakes and omissions will come to light with this trial run. Looking back on my notes on a trial run I find comments such as 're-arrange loco working at Deepwood to allow GWR loco to be turned at 1.34. Send out LNWR 4-4-2T to Viaduct Junction at commencement of timetable', and so on. Ask each operator to keep a note of the starting and finishing times or periods when he has nothing to do. This information will allow you to plan times for shunting up goods trains.

Although we have allocated the locomotives and carriages to trains, the make up of goods trains has yet to be tackled. Goods workings, are to my mind, the most interesting part of model railway operation. You can make this aspect as simple or as complicated as you wish. The simplest way is to leave the operator to shunt out whatever wagons he wishes to, in which case the only instruction needs to be to shunt up a freight train not exceeding 'x' number of wagons. 'X' is of course determined by the gradients, and therefore the haulage capacity of the locomotives, or by the storage capacity of the siding into which the train must run at the next station. As a first step this may be perfectly adequate but it will tend to get boring after a time. When boredom sets in it is high time to introduce more complex goods workings.

One more interesting method is to give each operator a detach/attach card similar to that shown at fig 11. The operator is instructed to make up a train from the wagons in his yard. He attaches the loco to the line of wagons in the first siding and starts with the first wagon. According to the first instruction on the attach/detach card he either retains the wagon for his train or detaches it and leaves it in the siding. Having worked through the first siding he proceeds to the second and subsequent sidings working down his attach/detach card. At the finish he has a string of wagons attached to his loco which form the outgoing train. Exactly the same procedure can be followed with an arriving goods train In this case the 'detach' wagons are placed in the siding and the 'attach' wagons are left to proceed on the same or a subsequent train. It will need some experimentation to find the correct ratio of 'attach' to 'detach' instructions for your layout. An alternative method, using the same idea is to use a pack of shuffled playing cards. You turn up one card for each truck, a red suit means 'attach' and a black suit means 'detach'.

Another way of adding interest is to allocate definite sidings for certain traffic. For example, one siding can be reserved for coal wagons, cattle trucks must go to the cattle dock, another siding reserved for oil tankers, and covered vans routed to the factory siding. The next step, especially where there are three or more stations is to prepare a 'routing card' for each goods vehicle. An example from our layout can be seen at fig 12. Here the wagon starts at Deepwood and has to be attached to a train going to Viaduct Junction. When the operator at Deepwood makes up a goods train for Viaduct Junction, he attaches the wagon to it and crosses out the name 'Deepwood' on the card. (Each routing card is covered with clear plastic and each operator has a wax pencil to cross through the relevant lines). When the goods train departs the operator hands all the routing cards for the vehicles in the train on to the next operator. He in turn removes all the vehicles marked to travel to his station and adds to it any wagons from his own sidings destined for stations further along the line. Once the operator has shunted the wagons which he removed from the train into the sidings, he crosses through his station on the routing card,and the wagon is ready to begin its next journey. This crossing through, will not be carried out, however, for wagons which are only in transit. For example, on our layout, a wagon going from Viaduct Junction to Sweet Hallow Valley would need to be detached from a Deepwood bound goods at Badgers Beach where it would have to wait for the next goods to Sweet Hallow Valley.

Fig 12

GOODS WAGON ROUTEING CARD

LMS Open Wagon No 21568

VIADUCT JUNCTION

VIADUCT JUNCTION — SWEET HALLOW VALLEY

SWEET HALLOW VALLEY — BADGERS BEACH

BADGERS BEACH — HEATHER HILL

HEATHER HILL — DEEPWOOD

With a large layout with several routes, there will be plenty of wagons which remain in a Goods Yard when a train travelling by a particular route departs, since many wagons will not want to travel in that direction, but with an end-to-end layout comprising two stations clearly the only routings would be from A to B and from B to A. In this case the routing card should be interspersed with instructions such as 'Stay in the goods yard when the next goods train departs'.

The card system has one fault, a definite pattern of movements which must be followed. That is, after going to Station A, the wagon always goes next to Station C, and so on. This is not very prototypical, apart from today's Company Block trains; the old fashioned goods van hardly ever followed the same route. One adaption of the card system that can prevent the same route pattern can be used on layouts where the stock remains in the same position from the end of one session to the beginning of the next. Cards are again prepared for all the wagons, but with just one list of all the stations or sidings on the layout. The layout controller notes that the siding at one particular station is nearly empty. This siding is, shall we say, the Deepwood Coal Merchant. The controller goes to the operator who works the Coal Mine Sidings and marks up three wagon cards to go to Deepwood Coal Yard. He gives these cards to the operator who shunts the wagons on to the first available goods train going to Deepwood. Likewise, when a siding is full the Controller can mark up some of the wagons in the siding to despatch them elsewhere; and then hand the cards to the operator for despatch in the first convenient train. This method will, of course, require a full time controller for all but the smallest layout, but it is an ideal job for someone who enjoys this aspect of model railways.

Further interest can be added to freight operation if you have a main marshalling yard through which all wagons have to be routed. If you have this situation you will probably need to employ the pack of cards technique for attaching and detaching wagons for departing goods train at each station. If you do not, it will just be a case of putting every wagon into the train, since all goods trains will be routed to the marshalling yard for sorting there into their different destinations.

When you are preparing your graph for goods workings, you will probably need to allow up to twenty minutes for a train to be prepared. Now if one operator is occupied for 20 min shunting you will probably find that other operators have nothing to do. It is no use leaving them in this state, for sure enough, they will wander over to a busy operator and start talking to him. This delays him, and so it goes on. I have found it best to keep each operator busy, even if it means that all operators are busy shunting goods trains at the same time.

After several weeks' operation of the timetable you may want to add a little variety. If you have some spare stock, try inserting the occasional special train. You will soon be able to find a route for these from your graph. Make up special instructions for these trains and issue these to the operators before the session starts. Another idea, if you have some double track, is to close one line for PW work. This will lead to another set of instructions giving train alteration times and perhaps some cancellations, together with the special rules for the operators concerned with working the single track.

There was a time when the timekeeping of British Rail left a lot to be desired. Why not introduce this facet to your layout occasionally? Give each terminus operator a pack of shuffled playing cards. When he has prepared a train for departure, he turns up a card. If it is a picture card he sends the train out on time, if it is a red card, say the 6 of hearts, he sends out the train six minutes early; if it is a black card, say the 3 of spades he send it out three minues late. To give the correct atmosphere, it is probably as well to remove most of the red cards!

By now, if you have followed all these instructions, you will have worked out a fairly comprehensive and interesting timetable which, I hope, will give your operators plenty to keep them happy. Perhaps, like me, you will find timetable construction an enjoyable occupation, or even at the worst, a necessary evil to enable you to provide the prototype atmosphere for your railway.

North Midland Railway

Photographs by
BRIAN MONAGHAN

Below: *A view of the main station on the layout — Tapton City*

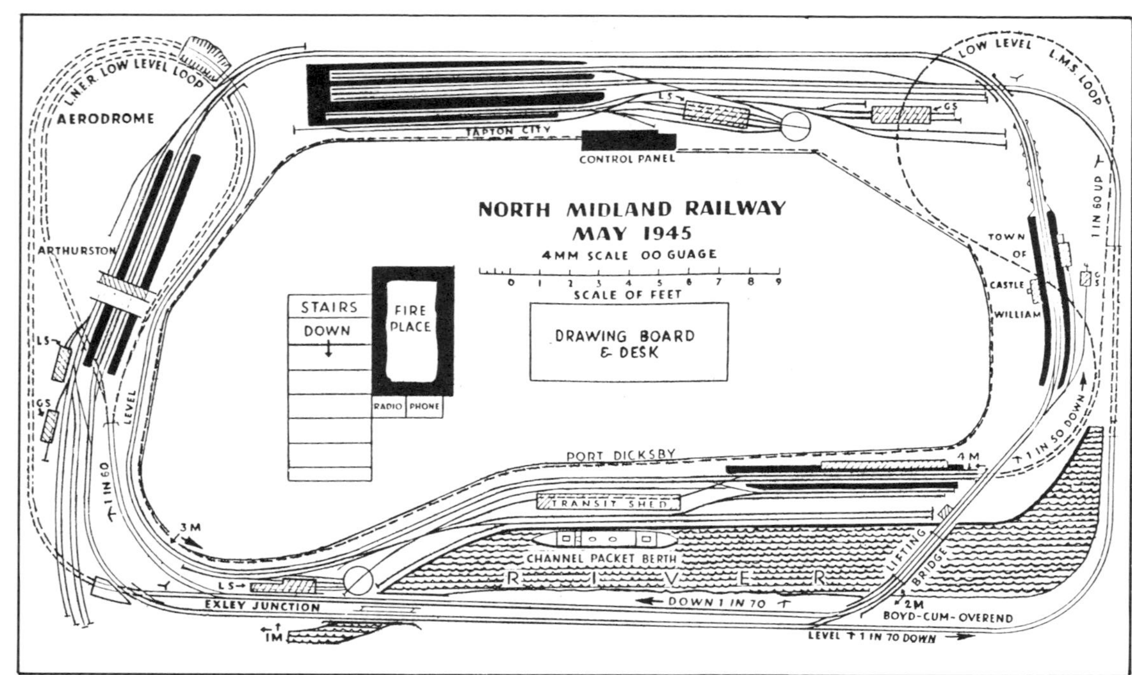

Left: *This view shows the uncluttered appearance and the space available for the docks at Port Dicksby.*

Right: *The turntable at the small motive power depot at Exley Junction near the Docks.*

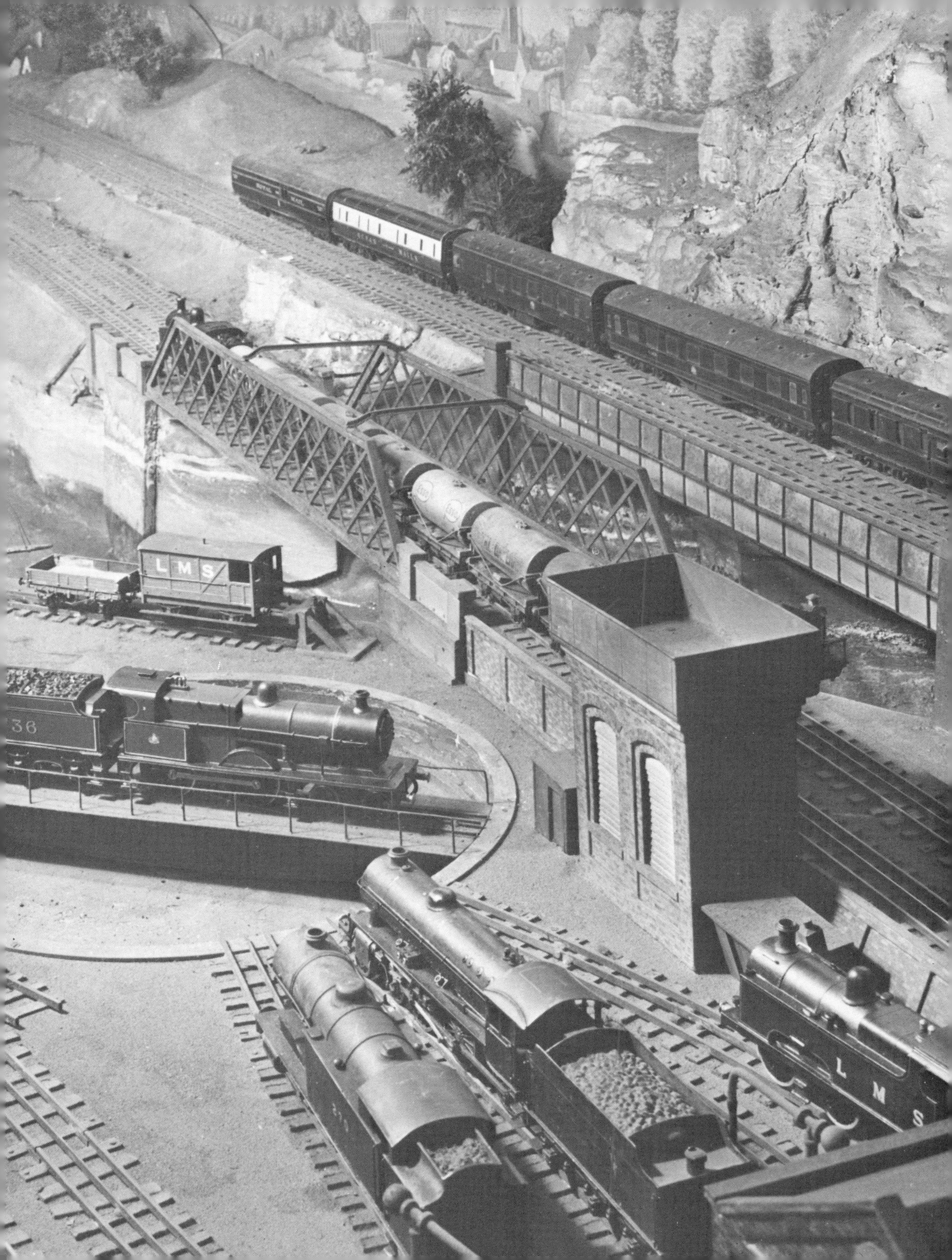
LMS
36
L M S

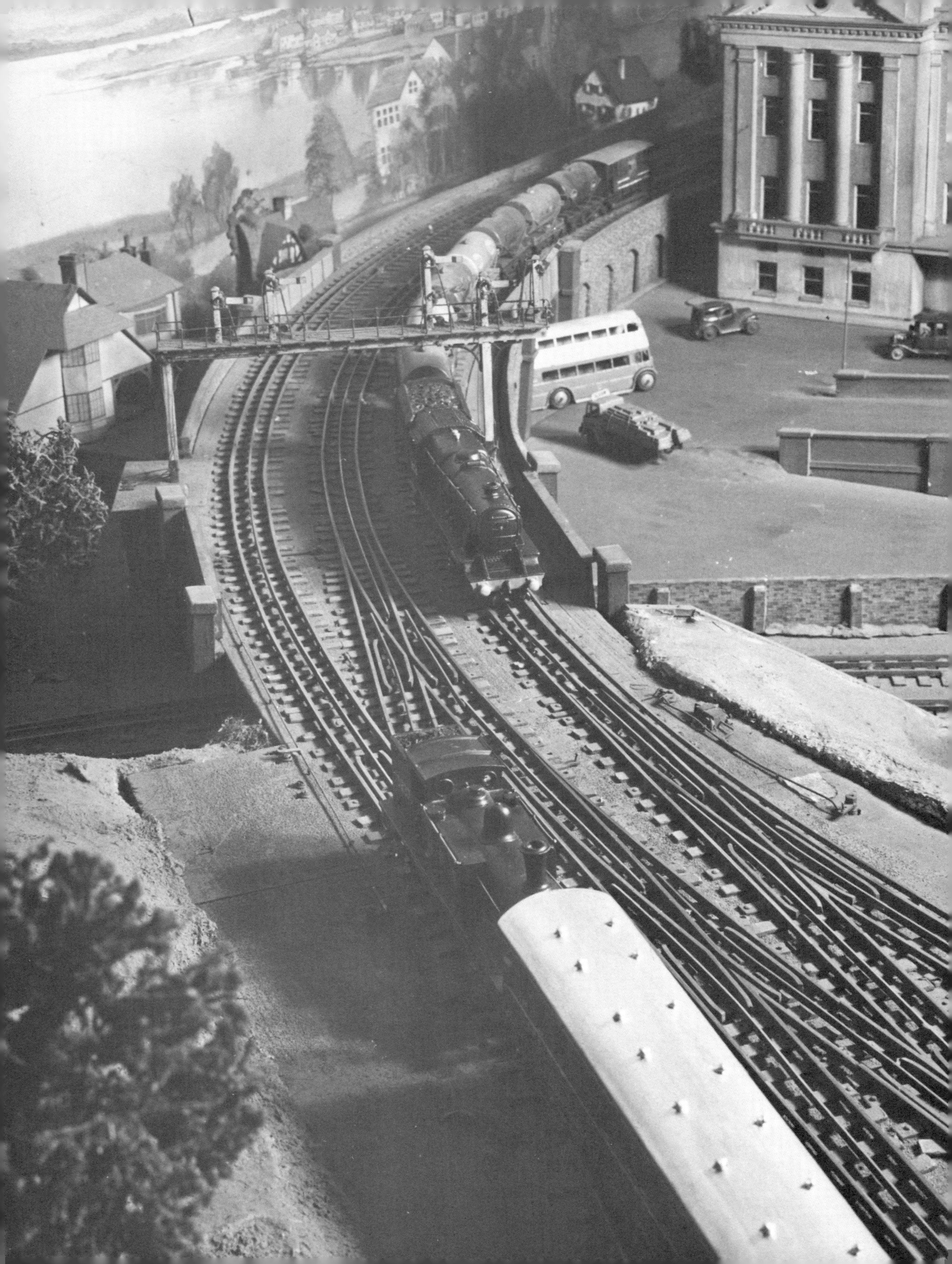

Left: *Part of the layout traversed the townscape and good use is made of actual model buildings and painted scenery.*

Right: *A view of Arthurston station with the goods shed and loco shed in the background.*

Below: *Interior view of Tapton City station.*

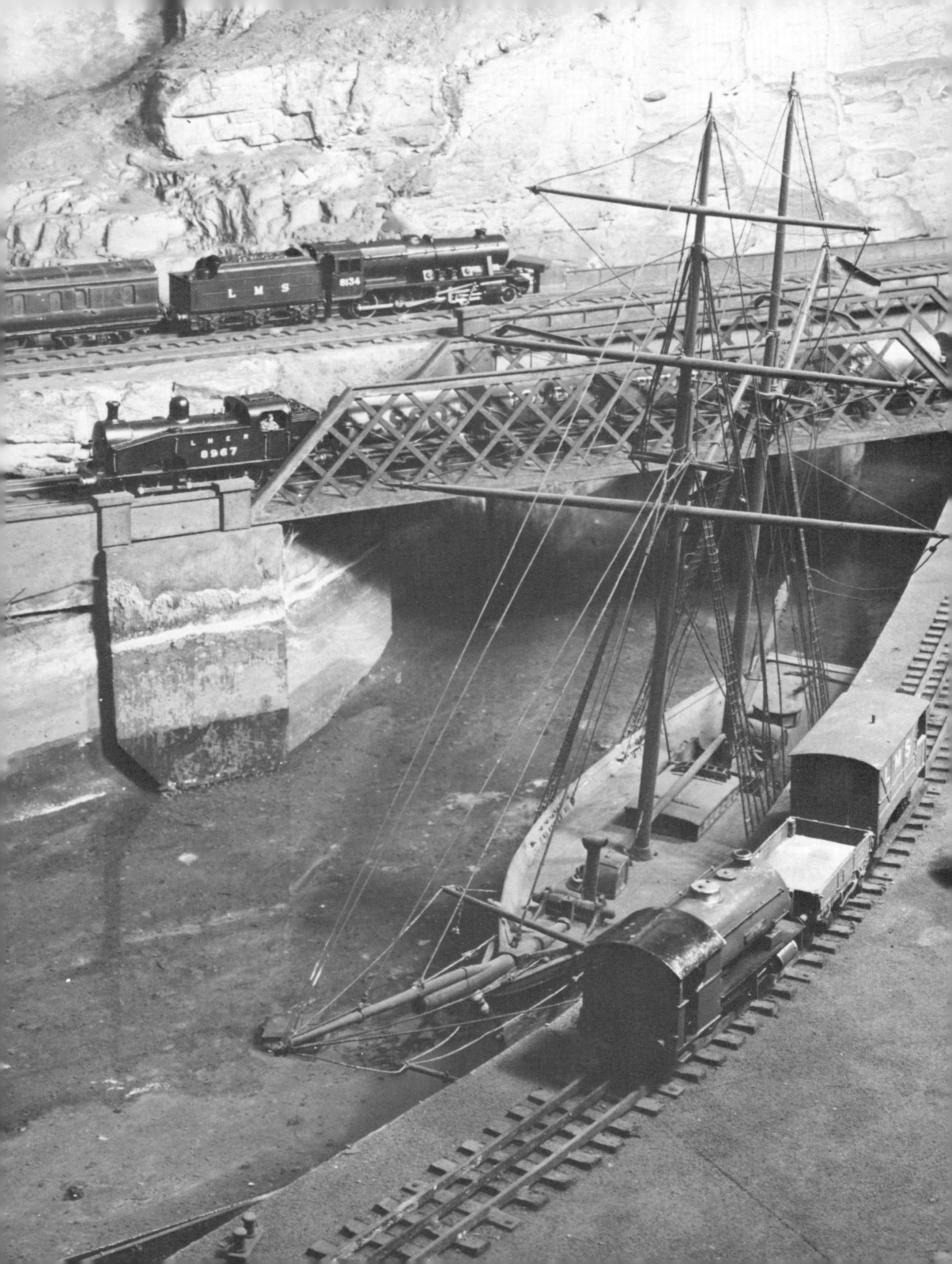
L M S
6134
L N E R
8967

Left: *A view of the railway bridge crossing the end of the Docks.*

Right: *A street scene alongside the railway at Castle William. The buildings and the vehicles are in keeping with the period portrayed by the railway.*

Below: *Exterior of Tapton City station.*

NORTH MIDLAND RAILWAY

Top left: *Exterior of Castle William station.*

Far left: *The cross-channel steamer alongside its berth at the docks. Note the Utility vans on the siding alongside the boat.*

Above: *Loco coaling plant at one of the mpds.*

Left: *The lifting bridge over the docks and part of the station at Port Dicksby.*

Notes on O gauge Loco construction

E. B. TROTTER

I have used Leeds Model Co's wheels for all the locomotives I have built, since the fact that they can be removed from their axles permits the dismantling of the mechanism for repair or painting of frames without having to have split bearings. With two or three exceptions Leeds mechanisms have been used, and it is a pity that neither the mechanism nor the wheels are now available.

Excluding one or two early attempts using clockwork mechanisms salvaged from old Hornby engines, my first gauge O locomotive was the ex-SE&CR class 01 which was built about 1948, as soon as LMC parts became available after the War. As it is an 0-6-0 it was only necessary to build a superstructure to fit over the mechanism.

Tinplate, which I had available, was used for most of the superstructure with the exception of platform angles, buffer beams and dummy front ends of the main frames, which required thicker material and are of 20 swg brass.

The sandboxes below the platform in front of the leading wheels were carved from hardwood and each attached to the underside of the platform by a small brass nail, the heads of which formed the filling caps.

A cast smokebox door was used on this model but, since then, I have often been unable to obtain the correct size and type of door and found they could quite easily be made from tinplate, the dishing being done in the following manner.

Two pieces of plywood about 2½in square are bolted together with a 4BA or similar sized bolt near each corner, and a hole the size of the door required is cut in both together with a fretsaw. The two are then separated and a piece of tinplate about 2in square put between the pieces of plywood, which are bolted together again. A length of hardwood about ¼in thick is cut to a width slightly less than the diameter of the hole in the plywood and the profile of the door cut on one end. This is then held on the tinplate and by tapping with a hammer and turning the hardwood a few degrees between each blow it will soon dish the tinplate to the profile cut on the end of the hardwood. The tinplate can then be removed and the surplus trimmed off. Tinplate or nickel-silver hinges, wire hand-rails and dart fasteners etc can then be fitted.

The construction of the rest of the body followed conventional practice, except for the boiler bands which, as in most other locomotives I have constructed, are strips of paper glued on with cellulose cement.

Since the tender springs on this class are above the platform, commercial axlebox/spring castings cannot be used. The tender frames are of brass drilled to take the axle ends. A hole drilled in the frame above the axle hole and filed almost square forms the top of the

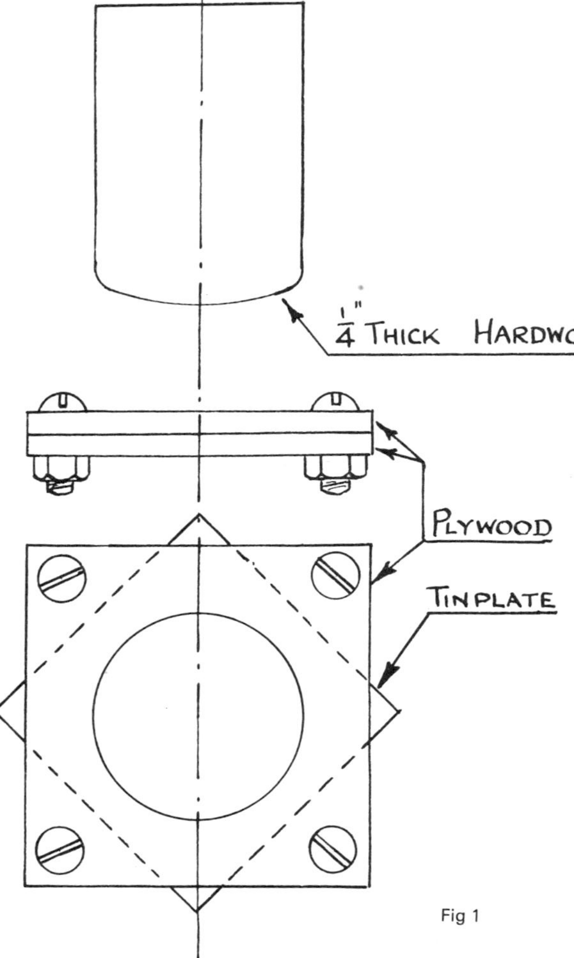

Fig 1

Above: *The completed model of the ex-SECR Class 01 0-6-0.*

horn gap, and the axleboxes were made from tinplate, cut and bent as shown in fig 2, and soldered to the frame. The springs, spring buckles and spring links were made from tinplate cut into strips of the correct width and bent as shown and soldered to the platform. Had brass or nickel silver strip of suitable width been available this would have been more suitable and saved much trouble cutting strips of equal width for the spring plates, but such sections were difficult to obtain at the time this engine was built.

As on all the other gauge O locomotives I have built the tender has the correct shaped tank and coal space, and a load of imitation coal (usually granulated cork) glued to a piece of plywood which fits in loosely so as to be removable, as is shown in fig 3. I have also provided a set of fire irons on each tender since a loco in service does not look right without them. Since details are probably not readily available to modellers a sketch of the ones generally carried on an engine are given in fig 4, the overall length generally being about 1ft to 1ft 6in longer than the firebox of the engine on which they are used. The pricker was made from 24 swg wire with one end bent at right angles in the vice and hammered flat, and the ring handles formed at the

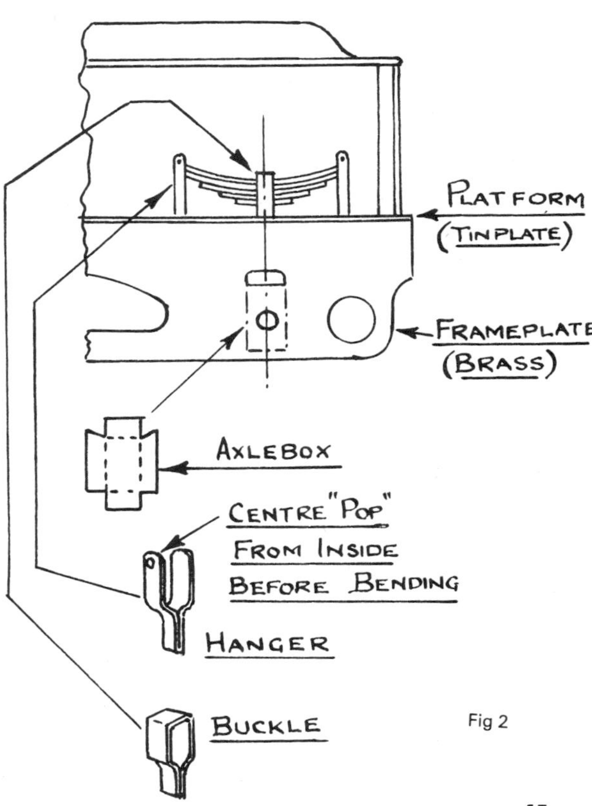

Fig 2

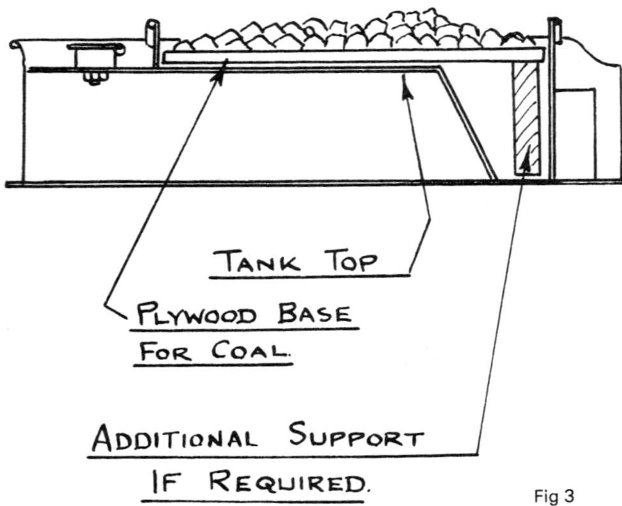

Fig 3

other end. The dart was also made from wire with the extreme end only flattened. The clinker shovel was bent up from tinplate with a wire handle soldered on. When completed they were all painted a rusty brown colour.

After completing the Class 01 I started on the J class 0-6-4T and the N class mogul. I really wanted an H class 0-4-4T since a layout representing the Eastern section of the Southern Railway would hardly be correct without one, but a conventional mechanism could not be fitted in such a model without completely spoiling its appearance. Separate motors small enough to fit out of sight between the tanks were not available at that time, and even if they had been, I would probably not have trusted my skill to have built the frames. However, I found that one of the standard Leeds Model Company mechanisms would fit in the J class with only very minor modifications, so that this was built as a second choice, construction being quite straight forward and requiring no comment, except that the piston tail rod covers, which project through the buffer beam, are long drawn hollow rivets, which have nicely domed ends and are available from many handicraft and leather shops.

The N class also has a Leeds mechanism and, since the firebox of this class of engine projects over the trailing coupled axle, the backplate of the firebox came behind the gearbox of the motor, and a full set of cab fittings could be added. The sight feed lubricator and vacuum ejector were filed from brass, and the larger copper pipes were made from suitable gauges of copper wire. Gauge glasses were cut from Perspex about ⅛in square and ¼in long and polished with metal polish. A 3/64in hole drilled through lengthways gives the impression of the glass tube within the protector glasses, and also provides the means ot attaching it to the firebox with a length of copper wire, the exposed parts of which suggest the gauge glass mountings. A sketch of one of these gauge glasses is shown in fig 5.

I decided to fit the pony truck with Cartazzi slides as on the actual loco, and this has proved quite successful although, no doubt, a lead weight would have been equally successful and much simpler but, at the time, I thought it best to make it as much like the actual engine as possible. This arrangement which, of course, also requires the pony truck to be sprung, is shown in fig 6. The side frames 'A' were made of brass and had tinplate axlebox guides 'B' soldered on. A radius bar 'C' was made from tinplate with the edges bent down for strength, as on the actual engine, and a trough shaped tinplate stretcher 'D' were soldered between the frames. The lower slide 'E' was filed from brass and made a good fit in the trough shaped stretcher. The upper slide 'F' was also filed from brass and has a recess in its upper surface made partly by

Fig 4

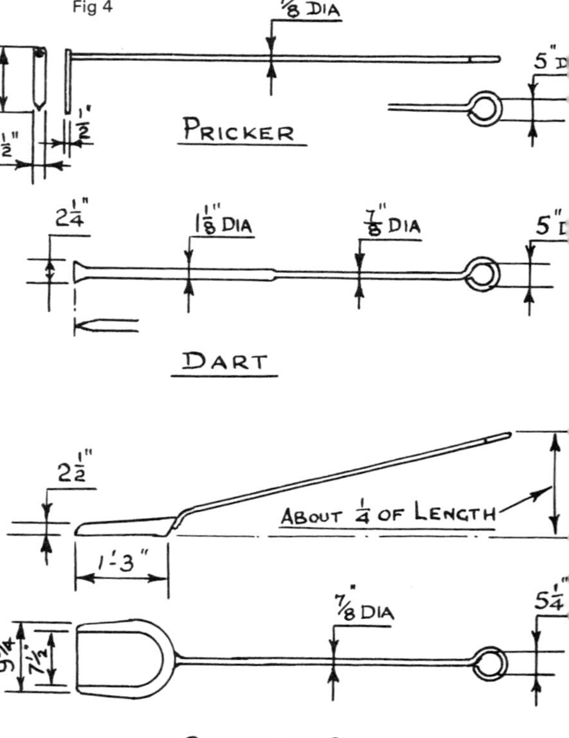

Fig 5

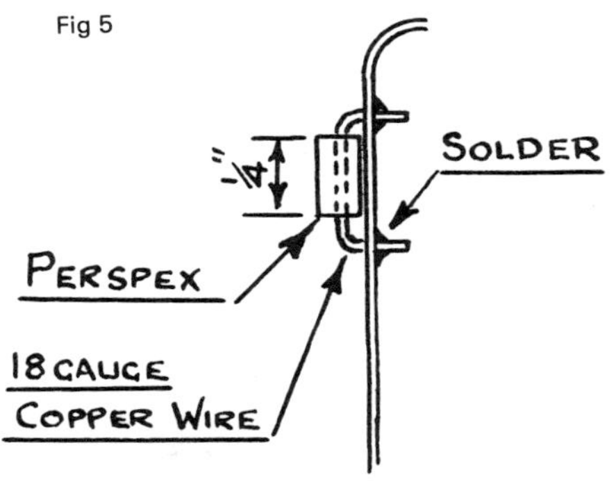

drilling and finished by squeezing a ball bearing into it in the vice. The ball bearing, 'G' in the diagram, was then soldered to a stretcher between the loco frames.

The axleboxes are also of brass, drilled to take the axle and with a blind hole in the top to take the pintle of the spring beam. The spring beam 'H' is a strip of tinplate with the ends bent to fit loosely round the 10BA spring bolts. The pintle is a short length of wire slotted to fit on the beam and soldered. After assembly, wire keeps were soldered across the horngaps in the frames to prevent the axleboxes falling out. On a curve the upper slide slides up the lower one further compressing the bearing springs so that these had to be very light to avoid lifting the leading coupled wheels off the rails. A strand from a stranded steel radio aerial was found to be suitable and the springs were wound from this.

Just before completing the model I soldered the return crank to the main crank pin, then found that without unsoldering I could not remove the connecting rod to get the mechanism out for oiling. I, therefore, adopted the arrangement shown in fig 7A of cutting two grooves in the crank pin to take a slotted return crank. However, I regarded this only as an expedient and on my other two locos with Walschaerts valve

Fig 6

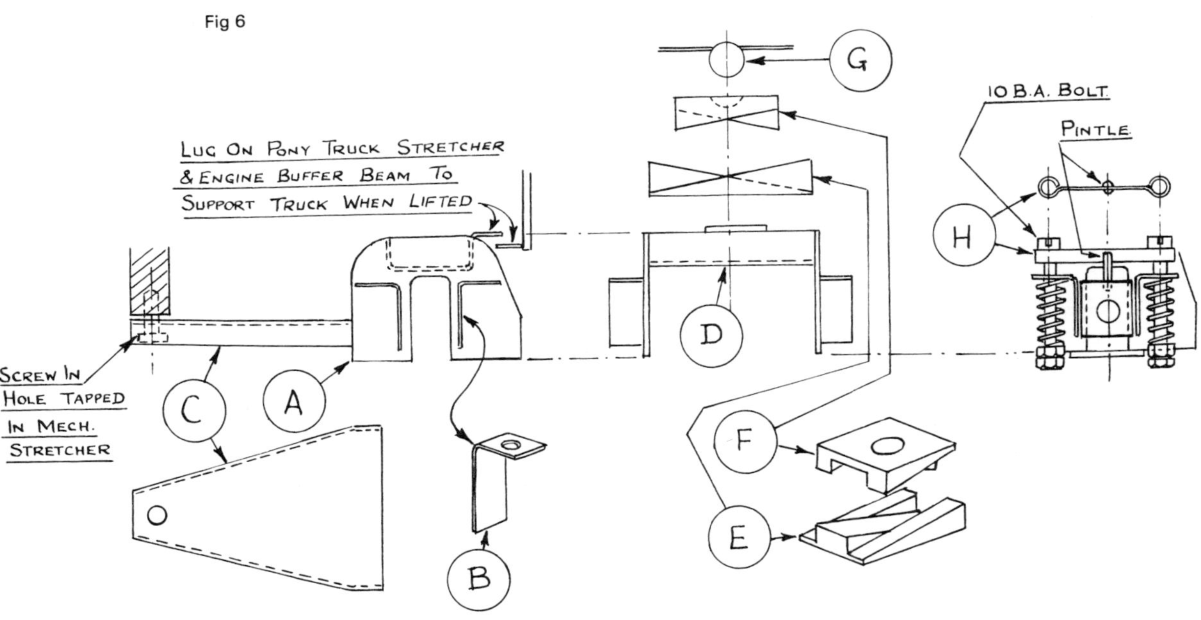

gear have let the coupling rods and connecting rod run on a length of tube and used a long bolt to hold the return crank and tube to the driving wheel, as shown at fig 7B. The head of the bolt for the 'Schools' class had an extra slot cut in it at right angles to the original one and the corners rounded off to give the impression of the four stud fastening used on the actual engines.

The D, D.1 and D.15 class 4-4-0s were built by conventional methods on Leeds Model Co mechanisms. The D.1 and D.15 have cab fittings, but the D class has a shorter firebox so that the mechanism projects into the cab as on the model of the 01 class.

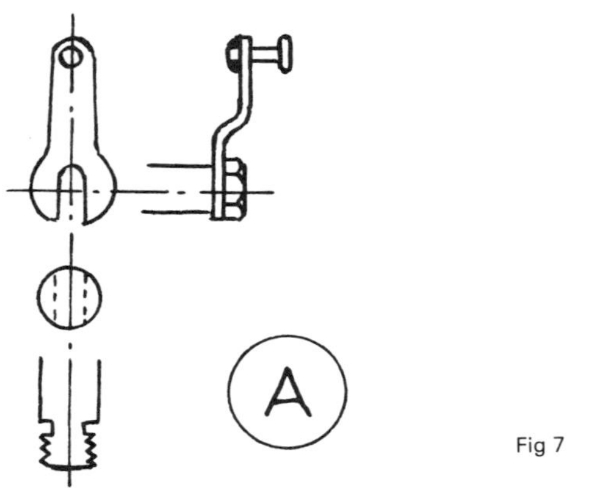

Fig 7

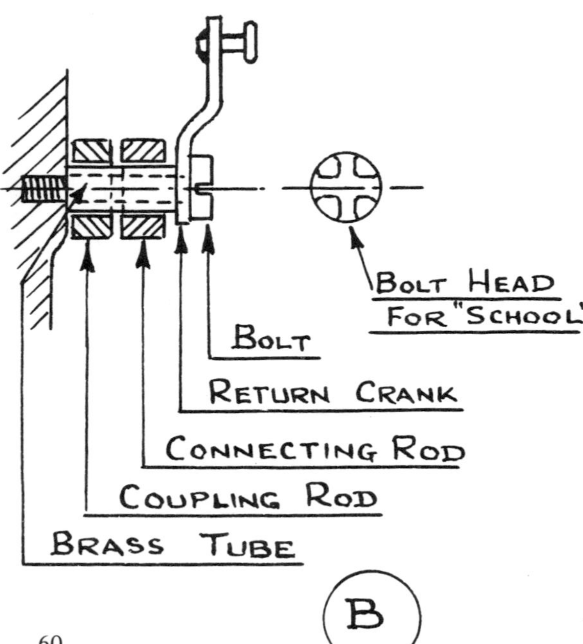

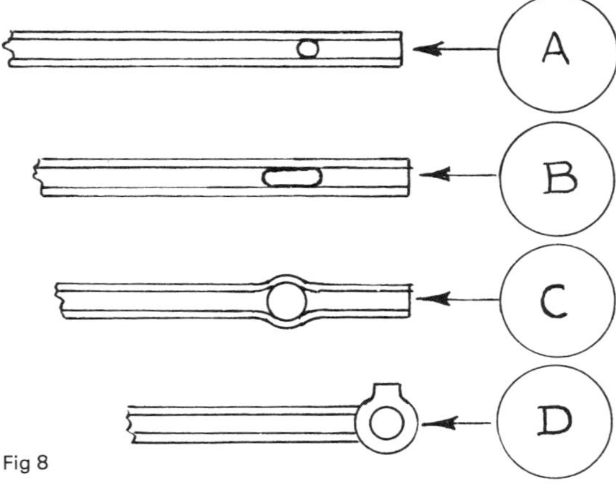

Fig 8

The King Arthur has full length brass frames to which the cylinders, slidebar brackets etc were attached, and is fitted with a Romford motor driving on the middle axle. Leeds Model Co wheels were used and the flanges retained on all coupled wheels, the trailing wheels being given a small amount of sideplay to permit taking a four foot radius curve.

The coupling and connecting rods were made from stainless steel which proved very laborious, and it was necessary to get a friend to make me a tungsten carbide tipped scraper to scrape out the flutes in the connecting rods. This loco required a number of handwheels for the cab fittings and the unsprung halves of Neweys snap fasteners were used. These are available from any haberdasher's in black or white, the latter, which are actually bright plated metal and can easily be soldered, should be used. Size 0000 were used for the injector stop valves, carriage warming valves etc, and size 2 for the reversing handwheel. The reversing wheels for the N class and Schools class were similarly made, but these engines have lever operated plug type injector stop valves so that very few small handwheels were required.

For the Schools class I again used a Leeds Model Co mechanism. The coupling rods supplied could not be drilled out large enough to take the brass tube used on the main crank pin so I made up new coupling rods, and the connecting rods, from steel bull head rail section then available from Bonds. Since the outside diameter of the brass bush was almost as great as the depth of the rail I drilled a small hole in the web of the rail (fig 8A), filed this into a slot as at fig 8B, then drove a tapered punch through making it like fig 8C. I had a sheet of softer stainless steel from which I cut end pieces which were soldered on as at fig 8D; a drill was then run through to clean out the hole to the proper size. The hole should not be drilled too near the end of the rail, otherwise driving the punch through may split it through the web. Having done the end for

Above: *The model of the SR Class N 2-6-0 with main line train emerging from a tunnel on the authors partly finished layout.*

Below: *A Southern Railway N class loco.* / Ian Allan Library

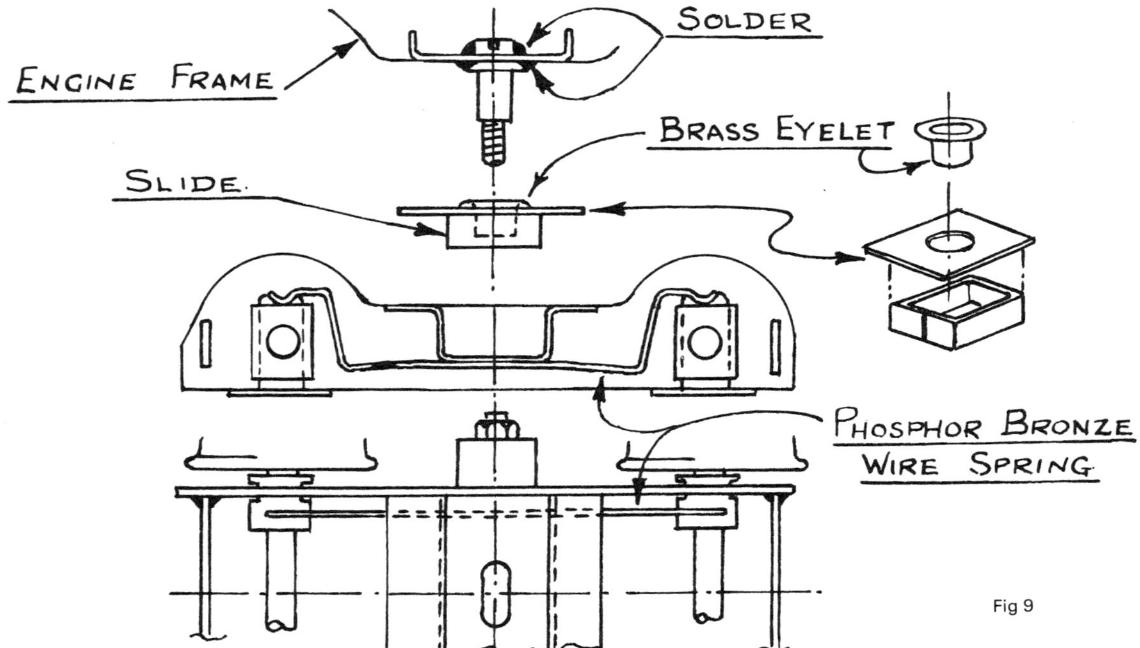

Fig 9

the driving crank pin, the position of the hole for the trailing crank pin was marked off. Since this pin does not require a brass bush, the size of the hole is small enough to be drilled in the web of the rail section without slotting and drifting.

Incidentally, I found the stainless steel quite easy to solder with Baker's Fluid, but impossible with Fluxite, and that the end pieces could be kept in position on the rail section while soldering by driving a match through the holes.

The bogie of the Schools class is sprung using the method shown in fig 9. The frames are of brass and the bogie stretcher was bent up from tinplate and soldered in position. The casing for the side control gear on the actual engine projects through a slot in the frame so that a dummy casing was soldered to the outside of the frame. The axleboxes were cut from ¼in thick brass and a saw cut was made on each side so as to slide in the bogie frame. The spring was made from phosphor bronze wire and soldered to the underside of the bogie stretcher. After assembling the bogie, strips were soldered across the bottom of the horngaps to prevent the axleboxes falling out. The slide consists of a rectangle of tinplate, with a strip bent to a rectangle soldered on to the underside. A brass eyelet soldered into a hole drilled in the rectangular piece forms the bearing. The centre pin consists of an 8BA bolt soldered to a stretcher between the loco frames and a long drawn hollow rivet of a suitable size to fit in the eyelet drilled through to fit over the bolt and soldered to the underside of the stretcher. I have used this type of centre pin on several models and, where space permits, have put a nut and lock-nut on the bolt below the bogie stretcher to prevent the bogie falling off if the engine is lifted. Where space is limited a blind nut can be made by soldering a small brass disc to an ordinary nut and, while this will not withstand excessive tightening, it can be tightened sufficiently to prevent falling off.

A few years ago I wanted a loco to work a push-and-pull set and, since no H class were fitted for this duty until about 1950, I decided to build an LCDR R class with an H class boiler as running in the Southern Railway period, and found that a Pittman DC 81 motor could be accommodated. This projected about ⅜in into the cab but came below the top of the tanks so that it is not very noticable, and permitted the fitting of regulator handle, water gauges and injector steam valves. Leeds Model Co wheels were used and a worm and worm gear obtained from Bonds. A local metal merchant had some ½in by 1/16in brass strip which was used for the frames. These were cut to shape and the holes for the driving and leading coupled axles drilled. Distance pieces were cut to fit between the frames in suitable positions for attachment of the body and to hold the motor. The motor was bolted to its distance pieces and the driving axle with gear put in position to ensure the distance pieces were exactly in the correct position, then the frames were cramped together with two cramps made from wood about ¾in thick as shown in fig 10.

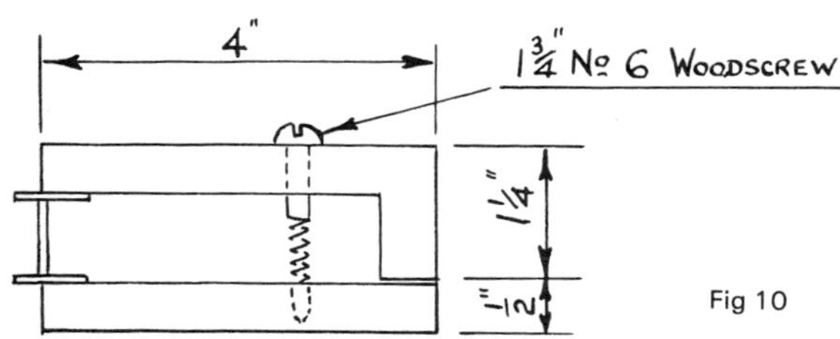

Fig 10

The motor was removed and the distance pieces soldered to the frames. The motor was replaced and the wheels fitted; coupling rods which, in this class, are not fluted being cut from 16 swg mild steel and varnished.

The bogie, which on the actual loco was of the equalised type, had brass frames made similarly to those of the Schools class, but set closer together to permit the fitting of the equalising beam (fig 11) outside the frames. The stretcher was made of brass of inverted 'U' section with a slot in it in which the centre pin, consisting of a bolt through a stretcher between the engine frame, fits. The slots in the side faces of the axleboxes were made nearer the inside, and a slot in the centre of the top locates the equalising beam. The bearing spring was bent to the shape shown from phosphor-bronze wire so that the ends hooked over the beam and the centre loop fitted on a bolt projecting from the bogie frame.

When the model was tried out it was found very prone to buffer locking at the bunker end, so the washer was soldered to the centre of the bogie stretcher so permitting no sideplay. The loco runs quite freely on my 4ft radius curves and the tendency to buffer locking has been considerably reduced, although, to be quite safe when running bunker leading propelling the push-and-pull unit, a plate with lugs is dropped across the buffers of the coach.

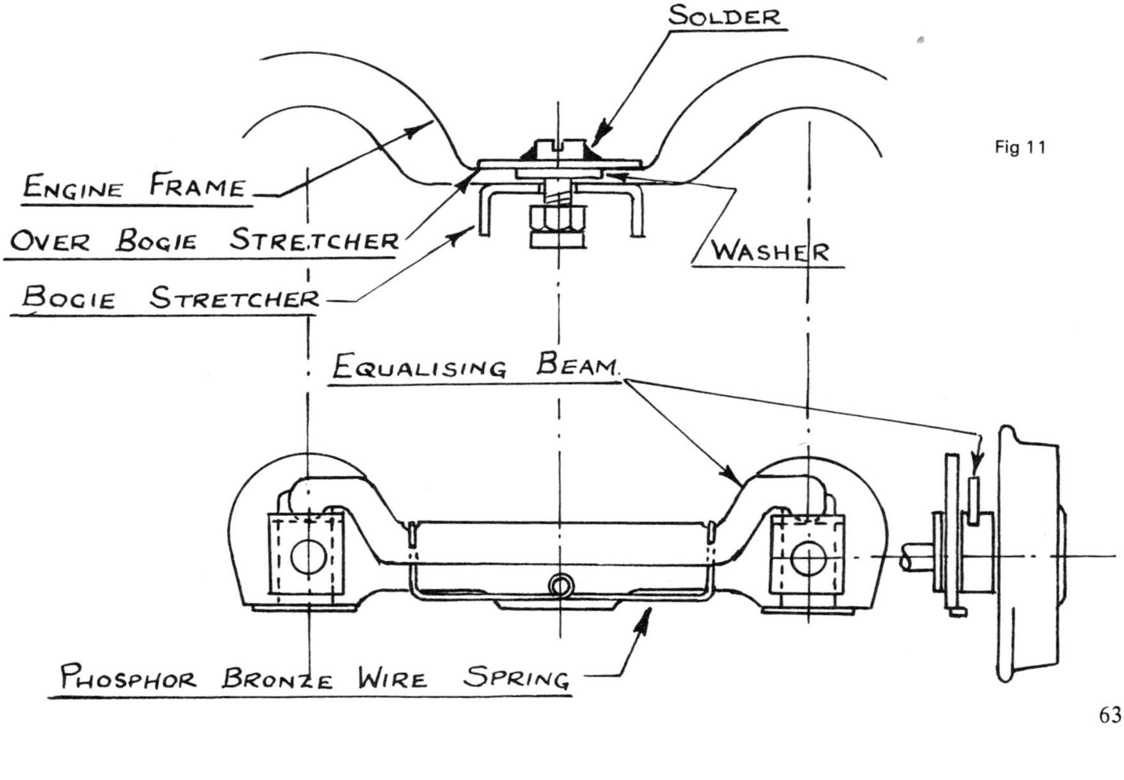

Solder
Engine Frame
Over Bogie Stretcher
Bogie Stretcher
Washer
Equalising Beam.
Phosphor Bronze Wire Spring

Fig 11

'It's a boy!'

Mrs G. L. HOARE

'Its a boy!' I settled back into my maternity pillows holding my first child — a son. This mysterious little bundle might turn out to be lots of things but one thing I knew for sure, he would be the 'The Reason' for my husband to begin on a life long ambition — a really super model railway.

We met when we were in High School. But while other girls had their first date in our Wiltshire country lanes, I was asked to 'come up and see my railway' which was what appeared to be a rather unweildy collection of O gauge shoved in an unwanted attic above the family bakery shop.

Now — things would be different. Of course he had to be patient and wait a reasonable time, at least until the toddler could say 'puff-puff'. So — plans were slowly formulated for a OO gauge railway which was to be in a small bedroom being prepared for our son Andrew.

This pioneer railway had two small stations and a moveable viaduct across the bed. The controls were on a bedside shelf. Trains could be run while actually laying in bed — a little boy's paradise — and Dad's!!

The grand opening was planned for Andrew's fourth Christmas. He knew there was something afoot because the small bedroom was kept locked and odd sawing and hammering noises came from there after he had gone to bed. We acquired a Tank Engine and an assortment of rolling stock and lined them up waiting for Christmas morning. Alas — the whole thing misfired! Andrew became so excited that he threw a massive attack of asthma. It was the doctor who carried him into the new warm bed and actually pressed the button to send the first train off on its exciting journey around the bedroom.

The bedroom railway was fun, but there were disadvantages — for instance — fluff from the blankets didn't improve the points and every time I bent over to 'tuck in', my rear managed to hit a cow on to the line, dismantle a signal or cause a major derailment.

For several years I had done my washing in a snug little shed near the back door. No mess or steam in the kitchen, everything to hand and convenient. I might have known what was coming. One evening my beloved bore down on me with eyes like engine head lamps — 'I want your shed!' It was no good to exercise women's 'lib'. Weakly I agreed to have STEAM (literal) in the kitchen while he made plans to have 'STEAM' (model railway) in my shed!

Since then my little shed has had two extensions. (Out of the question when *I* wanted to extend my utility ideas.) It now measures approximately 19ft by 7ft and houses — and let me quote a remark made by an enthusiast who visited us — 'one of the most adventurous little railway layouts in this area.'

Aided and abetted by my father who is a retired engine driver of some 50 years' experience, also a modest railway artist, the layout began. (I've just had a terrible thought, I wonder if I was married for my father's experience and expertise?)

The layout is mounted on a 2in by 1in framing of Sundela Board. There is a double tracked circle one on top of the other. The under circle has two loops.

First let me tell you what stock we have accumulated over the years. (You'll notice I've said 'we' — yes, I'm now a railway fan too!)

Now — the layout. The top circle consists of a four road through Junction station called Rode Junction (after a tiny village a few miles from us), with large marshalling yard and engine shed, turn table and coaling plant. There is one through station called Hemley, (so called because it was a collection of odd letters we had left over!) with a small sub shed and quarry sidings with crushing plant. At the Rode Junction a single line begins to climb up to a small terminus called Seaview (for obvious reasons) with goods yard, having passed Hemley halt on the way.

All main line points are electrically operated, the sidings in the yard being hand operated. The line has been signalled, using Ratio signals, without, however, any distant signals, save one, but so far it has not been possible to find a method to work these from the control point.

The line is controlled by 4 controllers — one each on each main line, one on the branch line and one for the marshalling yard engine shed. Yet, if required, the whole line can be controlled from any one of the controllers.

The scenic work takes various forms. My rather amateur attempts at background running scenery painted in poster colours on ordinary lining paper used for walls, with the more complicated things like a gas works pasted on! (I know when I'm beaten!)

My father made block scenery from Shredded Wheat cartons for the corners. This included some imposing cliffs with trees made from pieces of twig and dyed Loofa, and grassy patches made from sawdust dyed green. There is also a church and cemetery of cardboard (with tombstones) and small summer house affair made of logs (twigs).

Our old friend dyed Loofa filled in, in quite a few places for hedges and clumps of bushes, scattered here and there among the purchased model trees.

Other scenic work has been done using wire and Polyfiller coloured with poster colour so that in the event of chipping one is not left with a bald white spot. The line is ballasted with Peco ballast glued down with Casco cold water glue. The buildings are a mixture of Airfix kits and cardboard cutouts and scratch built.

Off the Branch line is a Dairy — a good excuse for using some six wheeled milk tanks. All the employees in the dairy (seen through the windows) looked extremely sunburnt. The reason for this is that they were Wild West 'Indians' bought up in a bargain bag of odd figures for a few pence. Painted in identical Dairy white coats they made ideal 'workers'.

At the back of the dairy is a long road leading up to the cemetery. This road has many pedestrians which also came out of the bargain bag and also a marching band in red and blue uniforms. The buildings on this road, which is against the wall of the shed, have largely been sliced in two, for economic reasons — only the fronts are needed.

Window cleaners, cyclists, postmen, policemen, mingle with various road vehicles and houses dwindle off here and there into country orchards with grazing cows and pigs and chickens.

My husband — as you may have gathered is a GWR enthusiast and his plan was to have an entirely GWR layout with one locomotive of each of the GWR classes which he can remember during his life time. A number of these models have been hand built by our friend Don Eve. All the other locos have been detailed and repainted.

Our son, Andrew — which was where it all began — is now married. His line is photographing the railway as well, now.

There is always some new idea to put into action, another little siding to be added . . . the railway is still developing after some twenty years — which is, I think you'll agree, the secret of the successful model railway.

6025	*King Henry 3rd*	4-6-0
2906	*Lady of Lynn*	
1022	*County of Northampton*	
4099	*Shooting Star*	
4906	*Bradford Hall*	
7803	*Barcote Manor*	4-6-0
4080	*Powderham Castle*	

47xx	4705	2-8-0
28xx	3825	
63xx	6302	2-6-0
26xx	2655	

3396	*Natal Colony* (Bulldog Class)	4-4-0
3800	*County of Middlesex* (County Class)	
3283	*Comet* (Duke Class)	
9017	Duke Dog	

4-6-0 2-8-0 2-6-0 4-4-0

72xx	7239	2-8-2T
42xx	4268	2-8-0T
45xx	4575	2-6-2T
81xx	8103	
56xx	5622	0-6-2T
14xx	1466	0-4-2T
54xx	5417	0-6-0T
57xx	5708	
94xx	9405	
22xx	2254	inside frame
23xx	2362	
23xx	2573	outside frame

In the coachline stock there is a rake of three GWR Dreadnought coaches handbuilt in Plastikard by our friend Mr Don Eve.

2 BSL 70ft
2 BSL 57ft
3 non-corridor clerestory coaches (Modified Tri-ang).
3 extended Tri-ang clerestories made into corridor coaches.
1 by 6 coach rake Centenary stock (Hand built by R. B. Wardle — my husband's boss now an enthusiast too).

K's autocoach
1 B set.
2 PC Coaches.
4 Syphon Gs.
2 Exley Full brakes.
2 Dean 40ft brake vans.
and over a hundred assorted Trix, Peco, Hornby, Tri-ang, Ratio and handbuilt goods vehicles.

Automatic Level Crossing

D. RANDALL

This level crossing is designed for a single line of railway, but could of course be used for a double track by using longer gates. It is made of oddments from the scrap box except that the gates and adjoining fencing happen to be from Airfix kits. It is also made to be worked by a hand lever but could be motorised by a suitable train of gearing. It is first necessary to determine the exact 'throw' of the gates, as both sides work together and the gates must clear each other as they cross the centre line.

To obtain this clearance the swivel posts are slightly staggered as shown in fig 1. As the line of railway in my own case is on a slight curve this enables the roadway to cross at a suitable angle. When the positions are found that enable the gates to open and close *together* without touching, holes for the gate swivel posts are drilled through the baseboard so that the posts project about ½in below, but this dimension is not critical. The posts are made from round brass rod (1½mm diameter) and the gates which are of plastic are secured to them by UHU or similar adhesive. Below the baseboard attached to the posts two operating arms of metal (a piece of scrap rail is suitable) are made and should be 1¼in long. To allow for adjustment a screw terminal is used to hold the operating arm to the post, the operating rod being soldered to this. At the outer end of the rod a small piece of tube is soldered. The central operating lever is made from either metal or fibre and hard wire is used to connect this lever to the gate post rods. The central operating rod is drilled as shown in the diagram and must be positioned according to the amount of throw

Fig 1

GATE CLOSED TO ROAD
FENCING
LINE OF RAILWAY
THROW OF GATES
FENCING
GATE CLOSED TO ROAD

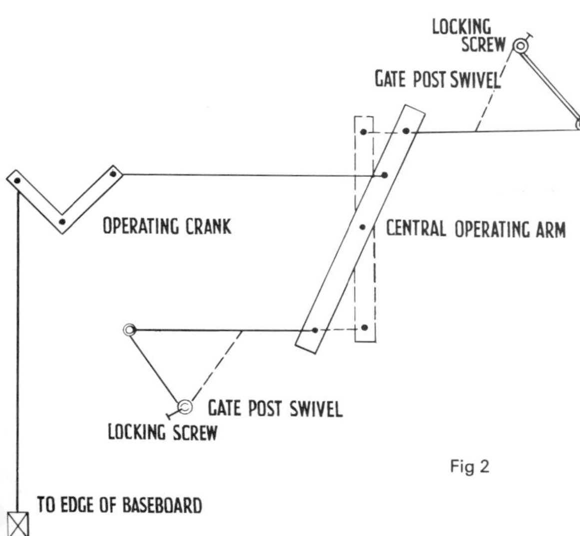

Fig 2

required which can vary as to the positions of the gates. An angle crank about three inches to the left or right of the central lever is connected as shown in fig 2: the other arm of the crank is connected to the operating handle as shown. It should be noted that the whole of the operating mechanism is out of sight under the baseboard. The roadway of the crossing is made partly by using the Airfix parts or other suitable material and a piece of black roofing felt is fixed between the running rails giving the appearance of an asphalted roadway. Strips of card to represent sleepers as used in other types of crossings could be used. Fencing either home made or proprietory is suitably placed to fence off the road and railway and so positioned that the gaps are entirely closed to either the road or railway according to the position of the gates. A lamp standard on each side of the gates and warning notices 'Beware of the trains' puts a finishing touch.

The OOn9 layout of the Merseyside MRS

Photographs by
BRIAN MONAGHAN

Below: *The Narrow Gauge layout represents a village in North Wales called Pen-y-Craig and this illustration shows how faithfully the atmosphere has been captured in miniature. Many of the buildings are copied from examples at Blaenau Festiniog and other places.*

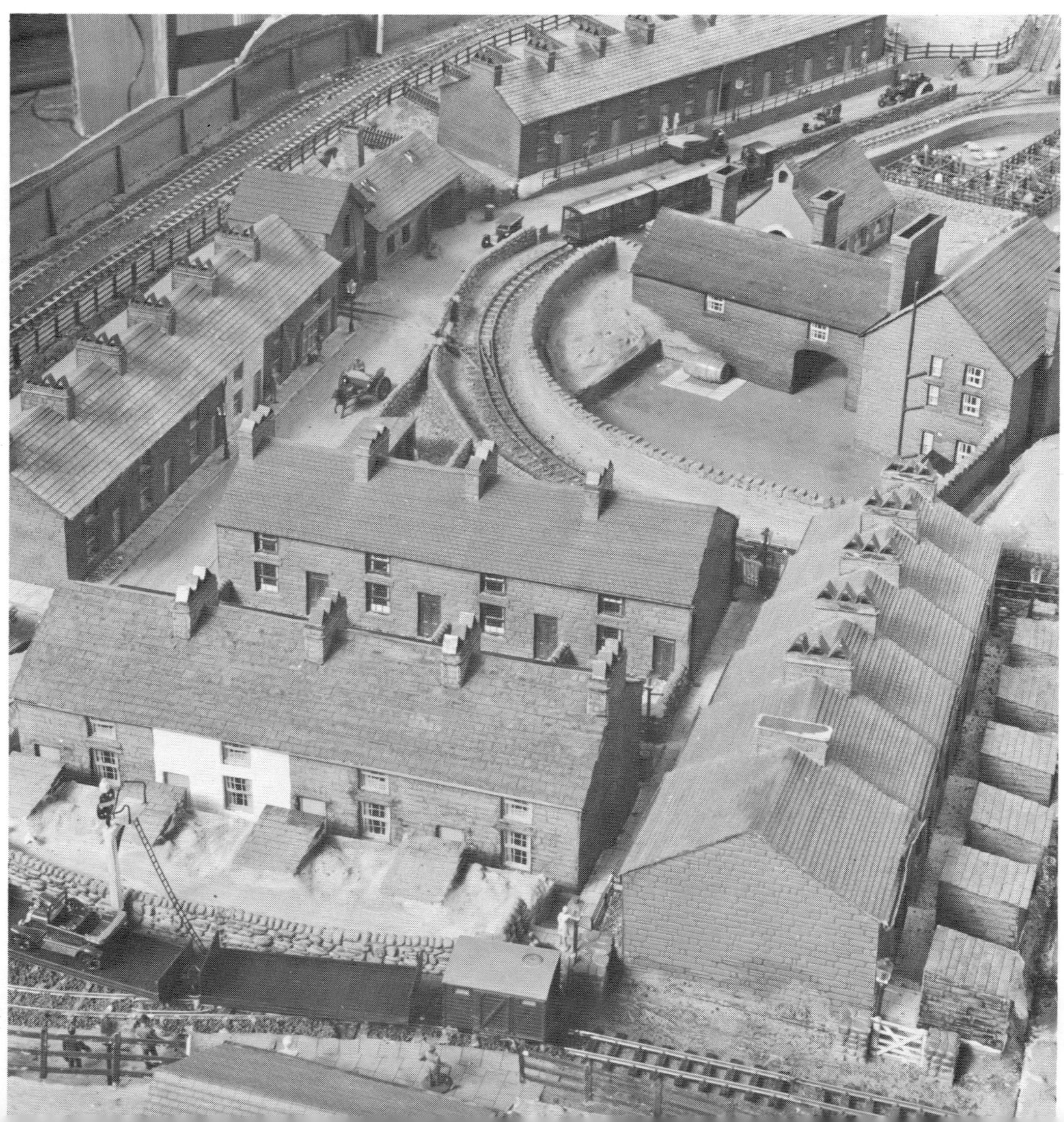

Above: *A double Fairlie loco proceeds through the town on its way to the station as another Narrow Gauge train in the background passes alongside the main street.*

Left: *The station of Llandrog near the slate quarry. Slate trucks can be seen ascending and descending the incline, with industrial trains running on both levels. These latter are mainly Playcraft or Eggerbahn models suitably adapted.*

Left: *A view at the other end of Llandrog station showing the quarry workings. Note the realistic appearance of the rolling stock and the derelict wagons above the workers coach on the left of the picture.*

Below: *A canal basin is incorporated on the layout and this shows the transfer sidings.*

Left: *A handbuilt loco traverses a bridge at the head of the canal basin.*

Below: The Chapel at Pen-y-Craig, which is also a market town and the sheep pens can be seen behind the chapel.

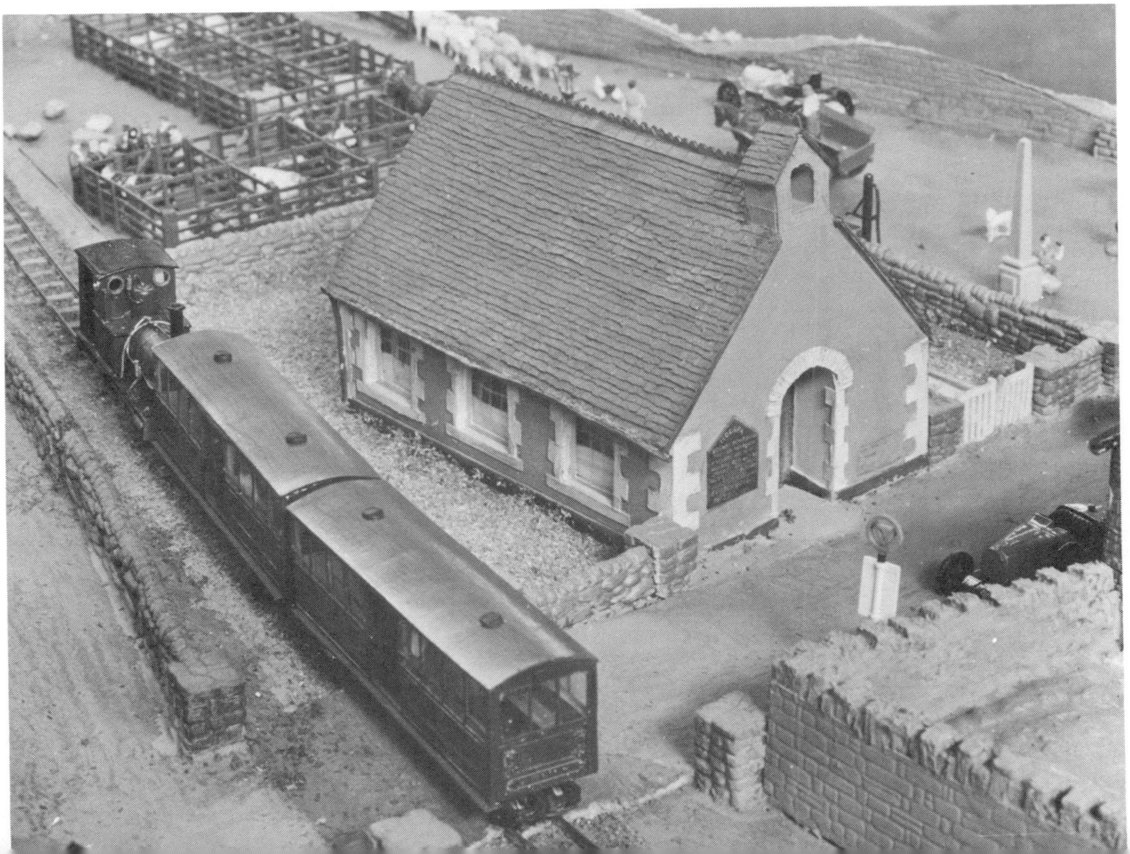

Above: *A Liliput HOn9 loco based on the prototypes as used on the Zillertalbahn in Austria. The coaches are a modification to a proprietary item.*

Top left: *Mountainous scenery is traversed by the railway and here a double Fairlie loco on a train of flat wagons winds its way along the valley.*

Left: *Realism and attention to detail makes it difficult to believe that this is a model. The railway station is in the background.*

Right: *A small maintenance depot for locos and rolling stock used in the quarry. The main line runs on the left which leads to the Llandrog station.*

Instant Action Accessories

IAIN G. A. HINES

Many otherwise excellent Model Railway layouts, seen either at Exhibitions or in private dwellings are somewhat marred, to my view anyway, by a complete lack of movement in everything, save the trains themselves. These chug along through miles of scale towns, forests and villages in which there is no activity to be seen whatsoever. Life is just not like that! If one goes on a bus or train journey one is confronted by a multitude of 'happenings'; people going about their daily routine driving vehicles, operating machinery which is itself seen to move, digging holes in roads, travelling in passenger transport so, there is nothing worse than to see a layout upon which a strange 'stillness' has settled, giving the effect of having been 'got at' by some fiendish foe of Dr Who who possesses a machine, which causes all life to stop dead in its tracks!

I think that this need not be so, if the layout constructor/operator would only use his imagination.

We are not yet advanced to the stage where we can operate an army of miniature people on our layouts, controlled from a master panel (but give us time!), however, perhaps the miniature people who do populate our layouts can be caused to be seen to be mobile, via their machines, which are quite easily controlled.

Thanks to firms such as Pola, Life-like, Tyco, Faller and Cox we can now acquire such items as operating freight depots, shanty crossings with moving occupants, freight trains with hoppers seen to be unloaded by miniature workers, operating logging mills, working fountains and a virtual host of other accessories guaranteed to liven up any model railway layout.

These items are realistic in appearance, easy to install and operate, and are really quite inexpensive. Perhaps one of the most important aspects in this day and age, is that they save construction time, giving us more time to spend on actual 'running' and doing such boring things as earning a living!

I have however personally found that they do not take much of the 'construction' enjoyment out of modelling. Far from it. Instead of constructing the individual items from scratch, with these instant accessories, I find one can devote more time to the actual planning of the layout. In other words, leave the construction work in other hands, and personally take the role of Town and Country Planner yourself! The possibilities are almost limitless.

For instance: One can now operate one's very own logging mill, operated manually by the 'flicking' of various levers, which cause the logs to roll down a hillside, on to a chute and into the Mill, from whence they can be rolled on to a log car, trackside. With a little imagination, and the use of another accessory, one can then have the logs transported to the saw mill, where they can be sawn up, then taken by road vehicles, of the Faller fully operating type to a factory, where they can be made into furniture, and delivered again by road to the retailers, or by container to distant parts!

The permutations possible, in such schemes are endless, with the accessories available today. The sets are not expensive, the logging mill for instance costing a mere £3.42 at the time we go to Press, that including the trackside flat log truck, an item which would surely cost £1.20 alone!

Many items are sold in separate units, which can be individually bought, then put together to form one major unit. The Faller quarry crusher set is a perfect example of this, the various parts being available separately, to enable one to buy them as the 'little lady', or 'old woman' (whichever the case may be!) doles out the weekly pocket money!

Having been motivated by various advertisements seen in *Model Railway Constructor,* I decided to look into the action accessory business a little, to see just what is available. I was quite amazed at what I discovered.

First of all, let us turn to a part of the Model layout which I consider to be as dead as the proverbial 'Dodo', the roadway, a part of layouts that my fiancee also finds most irritating! She just cannot understand why the cars don't move . . . well I've been thinking about this typical female statement . . . and must admit to wondering . . . well . . . why don't they? Now I know that some will say that we should only be concerned in the track vehicles themselves, but if that is so, why do we bother about anything else at all? Why not just run them around a bare base-board! The answer is of course, that we want to see our trains operate in a realistic model setting so, if that is the case why not do the job to the best of our ability, creating, wherever possible, an 'as near to real life' system that we can.

Above: *An HO model Carriage washing plant by Herpa and the brushes actually revolve and will clean dust and dirt off coaches. The HO scale accessory will take 4mm scale rolling stock as shown.*

Right: *A Tyco (American) working model of an ungated level crossing. As train approaches the crossing keepers small house is lit and signalman appears outside.*

So, back to the roadway, having answered that point. There is nothing worse than seeing our fantastic trains, move around our wonderful little layout, passing model roads on which stand idle vehicles, looking as though they were all awaiting the AA or RAC. These two organisations would really have their work 'cut-out' servicing the cars on the average model railway layout!

Shame on us for putting these two illustrious organisations to so much trouble, albeit in miniature. The alternative is quite easy, thanks to the model road system manufactured by Faller, and widely available in the UK.

This Faller system is just what is required to get that traffic moving, and can be quite easily incorporated in any model railway layout, being basically simple to operate.

A variety of road sections are available, which can be easily clipped together, and the tiny vehicles are a sheer delight, with their realistic finish and, in most cases, miniature occupants. They are controlled by a hand throttle which operates from a six button multipurpose control panel. One can simulate most road systems and conditions with this accessory, as various tracks sections can be obtained including a level crossing section, single-lane grade crossing, branch-offs and loops.

Complete sets are available, including the motor-rail set-up, with it's forward/reverse vehicles, throttle, track, control panel, ramp and motor-rail truck. With this set, one can of course incorporate a vehicle transportation service, a service which incidentally is becoming increasingly popular all over the World. The renowned American 'Auto-train' for instance, which runs from Washington to Florida has a three month waiting list! There is an HO scale version of this train, available from Bachmann, which could perhaps be incorporated within the Faller system, which costs £11.88 complete.

Another complete set available from Faller is the container terminal, which enables one to off-load container wagons from lorry or trackside. Premounted motors are included for raise/lower, sideways and forward/back functioning, along with other typical terminal features. This set is No 402 and can be incorporated with set No 406, the container lorry set, while both sets are combined in No 408.

Marvellous possibilities then with these miniature road systems and there is no longer any need for the miniature RAC and AA to be called out!

Faller also manufacture an extensive range of other accessories, including such items as the Black Forest sawmill, with motor-driven saw, a Watermill operated by water and a small 12-16V pump, an ornamental fountain gushing forth water, a moving Windmill as well as lighting sets to light up the model buildings. The Church Bell system is also one of my favourites, a really nice sound to be added to the sound of the trains, but bats are emphatically not supplied. I sometimes think that we model railway enthusiasts have quite enough of them!

Tyco of Woodbury Heights, USA, formerly the renowned 'Mantua Metal Company' are now beginning to have their products seen in the UK, at various retailers, so are worthy of mention especially in view of their range of exciting accessories which always, somehow or other, seem to make me laugh! No offence to Tyco, I think it is the realism of the situations in which their operating accessories appear that make me chuckle, and in these troubled times that can't be bad!

For instance. Imagine one's model train approaching a level crossing . . . by the crossing is a small dimly lit shanty, in which, apparently, sits the shanty keeper . . . what's that? . . . the shanty door is opening and old Ebenezer McDoakes comes out, lantern in hand, disappearing back into the shanty for his cuppa cawfee only when the last carriage or caboose has cleared. Unbelievable? Not at all. I have just described the action of Tyco accessory No 928. At a cost of only nine dollars in the USA this one would if other Tyco Import prices are anything to go by, sell in the UK for around £3.50.

Set No 930 is just as good. A freight car approaches the freight depot. It stops adjacent to the unloading platform. The door of the car opens, and Ebenezer's son appears and is seen to throw the freight boxes and cases out through the door, on to the platform receiving bin. Get the idea? Or how about No 931? Ebenezer's son-in-law Joe Soap is sitting at the controls of his pipe unloader tractor, dreaming of his wife's Apple Pie. All of a sudden a flat car approaches, carrying culvert pipes. As the car draws level and stops, the arm of Joe's tractor extends as he drives the tractor forward, gently tips the pipes from the car on to a ramp and Joe returns from whence he came, being careful to miss the little houndawg sitting on the platform scratching for fleas.

These Tyco offerings, are quite good and many more are offered, including a piggy-back loader, an operating floodlight car, hopper unloading set and the magnificent crane car, with boom tender and operating railborne crane.

No work is required on any of these items as they all come completely finished . . . well, perhaps a little weathering, just to keep the old eye in!

The American 'Life Like' company manufacture some nice accessories and, as I mentioned before, the one that really 'caught my eye' was the logging mill set. A really realistic little model this one, requiring only a little weathering. Life-Like also manufacture the Tracksider buildings, and for anyone modelling the early West (a period for which there are some great items available), then their Cripple Creek watering hole, Interlocking Tower, Expo-Express Company Freight shed and Timberneck Gulch depot and freight platform should see you alright.

While on the subject of the Golden West, this is I feel, a period not often covered in this Country amongst American outline operators, yet there are many wonderful items available, with which to portray the period, from the wonderful locomotives by Tyco and Rivarossi to the buildings by Bachmann and Life-Like, miniature people being easily obtainable, one of the Airfix sets being particularly suited, (Wagons West I believe it is called).

Another American Company manufacturing accessories of the action type is Cox of Santa Ana, California, famous for its range of gas-powered vehicles and aircraft. They have already entered the HO world of model locomotives and rolling stock, but in 1975, also entered the accessory field with their Trainscapes.

These look very interesting indeed, and there are to be a large assortment available, taking in all manner of situations, from the Dockside train sets, with a freighter, F3 loco, dockside platform, two truck container loads, three crates, two Oil Drum pallets and track included, to the Dockside conveyor set, with unique operating belt. They have also gone into the 'logging business' with their various Big Pine lumber and sawmill sets.

There is also a military train, modelled on a typical US Army train, called The GI General.

Many of the firms mentioned within my article also manufacture pre-formed layouts, which are chiefly aimed at the railway modeller who has not even enough time to construct his own base-board. They come ready-flocked and are manufactured from high-impact styrene, and one's sole job is to lay the track and buildings, although some British retailers even provide this service. I saw some recently at the Euro Show at the Central Hall, Westminster and was amazed to see that they cost around £200, amazed that was until I totted up the cost of the items on the board individually, it wasn't far short, allowing for labour costs! These units can even be joined to form much larger layouts. I note that Faller indeed have released one, upon which their Quarry Crusher can be installed.

These various landscapes are manufactured by Kibri, Noch and Faller.

Really, when one considers it, imagination is the key word when planning one's action accessories.

For instance, the Subbuteo football game, which is to HO 'scale' and which features football figures, press

Above: *Hornby Railways operating travelling post office set which picks up mailbags while on the move.*

box and figures, a TV Camera team, floodlights, linesmen, a ref, score indicator, in fact everything which is to be found at a real football ground. It would, I'm sure, make a fascinating accessory to a model railway layout. The floodlights actually work and the complete set could perhaps be installed at the edge of the layout, with a Soccer special, (constructed and put together from one's tattiest coaches) serving the ground! (Such is life today unfortunately).

Another scenic which is not often seen on a layout is an Airport. This is quite surprising, as today there are many suitable model aircraft, airport vehicles and airport buildings available. I am not suggesting for one moment that one should have Heathrow in one's drawing room, featured on the layout, but a small country airport would surely be possible, with a small flying club present, or, if the layout would take a *bit* more than that, then a small RAF Station.

We oft-times go astray when it comes to putting miniature figures upon the layout, too. How often do we see figures standing in the middle of the road on a large slab of concrete, or rather what appears to be one, figures on a platform, facing anything at all but a fellow human being, here again, nearly always standing on a large slab of con . . . (here I must really get something off my chest!! Why do we persist in leaving the stands on our figures. It is surely easy to cut them off and stick the figures in place by some alternative means.)

Surely, having spent such a long time putting a layout together we could spend a little more time with the figures? Perhaps we don't do so, because we 'can't wait to get rolling'. Yet a little more thought and a little more time spent on this important job would make such a difference as far as realism is concerned.

Why have everyone standing stiff, anywhere as long as it's somewhere, gazing into the wide blue yonder, interested in nothing that's going on around him? Let's add a little realism!

Look at that dog running down the street, with a string of sausages in its mouth, and look, look, the Butcher boy is chasing him! . . . see Mrs Smith hanging out her washing again, hope it doesn't rain . . . there's the Vicar passing the School on his bike . . . see it's the kiddies' playtime. That nosy woman at No 16 is hanging out of her window again and . . . my Gawd!! . . . the Soccer special's just arrived at the Station, lock up your daughters!

All of this is possible, with a bit more time and thought spent. I remember one model railway exhibition where a layout featured a Quarry upon which the most unbelievable events were taking place. I had to go back four times before I saw everything, and I noted that it was most probably the most popular Exhibit.

People don't want to only see the trains, they like to see other things too, just ask them!

Also, the incorporation of operating accessories on the layout ensures that the whole family, or Club has a crack of the whip regarding actually actively doing something! I personally would love, some time, to build a layout upon which there would be all manner of operating accessories, each requiring an individual operator, and this would mean that the layout would not be, as layouts often are, a 'one man show'. Whilst one operator worked the Quarry, another would work dockside, whilst my two boys would most probably be happy to see in the Soccer special, and play the actual game.

I don't suppose for one moment that this article will particularly attract the 'purists' in any way, but, in all honesty, I feel sometimes as though I am a voice, 'crying out in the wilderness' as far as some aspects of our wonderful hobby are concerned. In particular, I feel that we are often guilty of being far too serious about it, that there is much more fun to be had by relaxing a little in our outlook. Why not try it! Who knows, it may be of immense benefit, after all, 1:1 life is serious enough these days, without carrying it into our hobby!

'Bury Hill'

The N gauge layout of the Bristol East (Downend) MRC

Photographs by
BRIAN MONAGHAN

Below: *An aerial view of the village and station. This shows the realism and detail incorporated in the layout.*

Left: *Part of the station area near the village of Bury Hill.*

Below: *View of the village and station.*

Above: *A main line train crossing the river bridge with part of Frenchy Mill in the background. The diesel hydraulic loco* Western Regent *has a handbuilt body by Bob Bones, a club member, mounted on an Atlas chassis.*

Left: *Another view of Frenchy Mill and the river.*

Right: *Two diesel hauled trains about to pass in opposite directions on the main line. A diesel shunter is on the private siding which serves Ash's Timber Yard, clearly seen in this illustration.*

ASH
ASH

Above: *An express freight train hauled by a GWR 'County' class 4-6-0 rounds the sharp curve past Wrigley's Quarry where loaded stone wagons are being withdrawn from under the loading chutes by an 0-6-0PT.*

Right: *Another view of Wrigley's Quarry noting the realism obtained. The train of stone carrying wagons is hauled by an SR Q1 class 0-6-0 built by Ken Woodroff.*

Left: *A repainted Peco N gauge Jubilee loco brings a main line train out of the twin tunnels.*

South for Moonshine

A 4mm scale SR Layout

S. W. STEVENS-STRATTEN

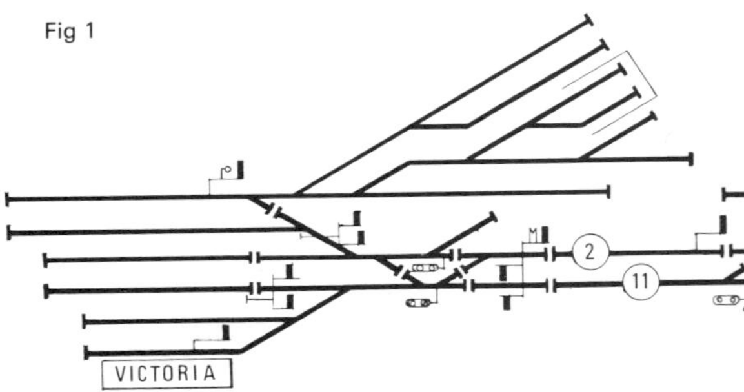

The layout had a purpose, trains were run not just for the sake of running them, but to fulfil an imaginative plan that made sense. The layout portrayed the Southern, and was designed to be a representation — but not, of course, a model — of the main Brighton Line from Victoria, with various Central and South-Eastern ramifications. This allowed for a wide range of SR trains which could be scheduled to leave Victoria at prototype departure times for many real, but mostly unmodelled, destinations. And the modelled part of the system was long enough to allow express running while also giving ample scope for crawling about in yards.

The General Scheme

Fig 1 gives a schematic diagram of the route, which provided end-to-end local running between Victoria and Reigate as well as out-and-back main line runs via the double-track return loop — where lurk a chain of seaside towns from Margate round to Portsmouth, and several inland places too. The plan (fig 2) shows how all this was accommodated within the space available, namely the garage.

It will be seen that the route was coiled round on itself on two levels, with the return loop concealed under Victoria. The outer track, descending most of the way at 1 in 80, also passed under Victoria before emerging at East Croydon as the inner circuit, which was level. Most of the line was on open curves, the longest continuous straights being little more than a full train length, while the track through Reigate Junction and the cutting beyond it was a long, wide-radius reverse curve leading out of an ample transition from the door end-curve. So trains were constantly changing their shape as they ran round the line, and never got dull, while the long tunnels under Victoria added a touch of mystery and disguise. The distance between stations was about three-quarters of a lap, so even with a stopping train there was plenty of room to build up smoothly to cruising speed and to maintain that speed for a reasonable time before slowing down to an unhurried halt.

At Victoria there were five platforms, of which the inner three represented the Brighton side of the station. The other two, together with the shunting roads and shed area, were mainly for South-Eastern traffic. The station throat was on 5ft to 8ft radius, with short lengths of 3ft. At Clapham Junction, only the up and

Right: *The station throat at Victoria*

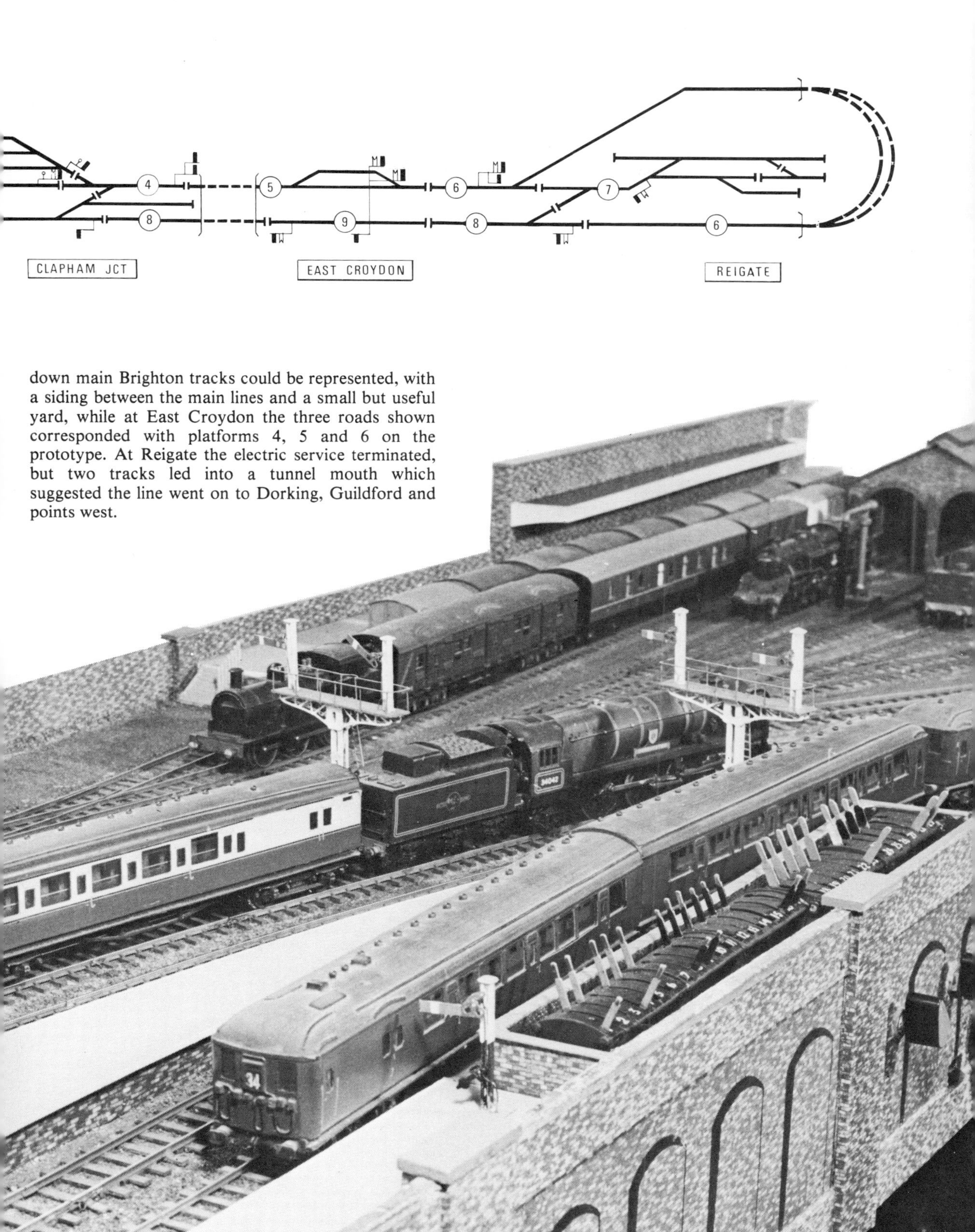

down main Brighton tracks could be represented, with a siding between the main lines and a small but useful yard, while at East Croydon the three roads shown corresponded with platforms 4, 5 and 6 on the prototype. At Reigate the electric service terminated, but two tracks led into a tunnel mouth which suggested the line went on to Dorking, Guildford and points west.

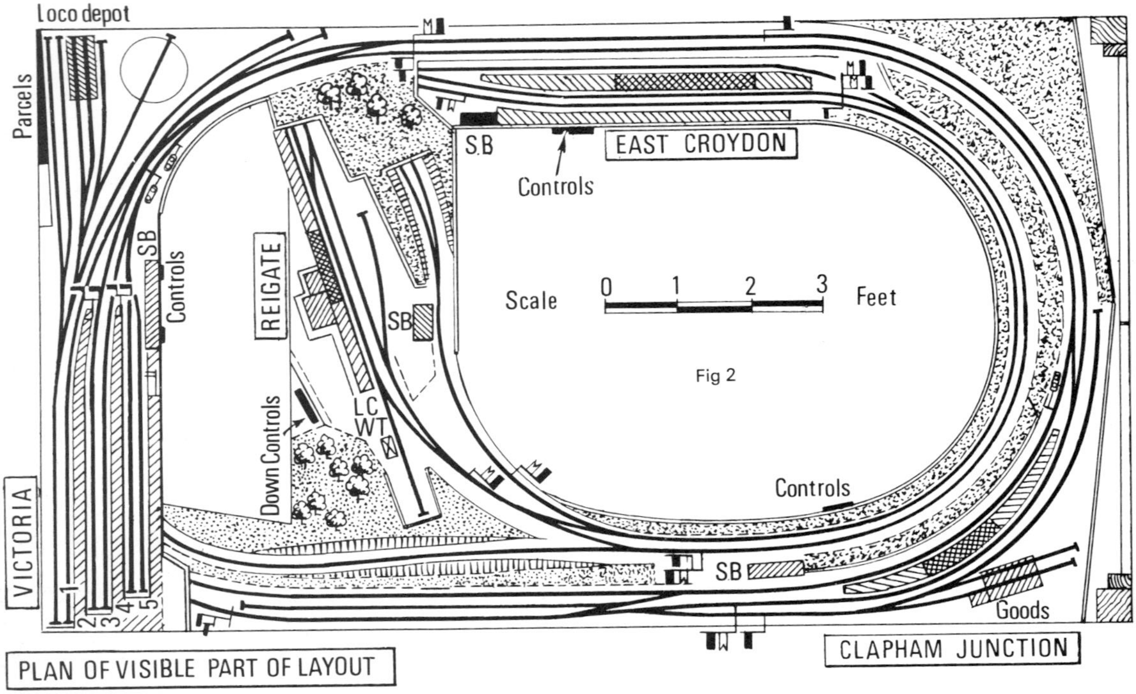

Loco depot
Parcels
SB
Controls
REIGATE
S.B
EAST CROYDON
Controls
Scale 0 1 2 3 Feet
Fig 2
SB
LC
WT
Down Controls
VICTORIA
1 2 3 4 5
SB
Controls
Goods
CLAPHAM JUNCTION
DOORS
PLAN OF VISIBLE PART OF LAYOUT

The Carpentry

The baseboards (lettered A to L on fig 3) were of hardboard or Sundeala, braced by the lightest battens that would give enough strength where wanted, coupled with a crosswise flexibility that would inhibit any powerful warping. A to D, and I to L, were supported either by wall-blocks and triangulated brackets or by the ends of adjacent boards, but E, F and G hinge up to allow access for the car, the bonnet of which passes beneath the Reigate board. To ensure that the hinging boards always mate up with their neighbours piano hinge cut into 4in lengths was used; one flap was screwed to a 1in thick block Rawlplugged to the wall, and the other flap was split so that one half could be screwed to one baseboard and the other to its neighbour. Thus both of them rotated about a common axis and could not get misaligned. The narrow end of G was supported by a spring-loaded sliding strut, and the wide end had a drilled lug that engaged with a pin in H. When G was raised, it locked into a simple gravity-operated latch on the wall, but E and F, which were heavier, were counterpoised and open like the Tower Bridge — see fig 4. There were safety contacts in the common return which prevented anything from running outside Victoria unless the bridges were fully down.

The hinging sections involved 80 rail-ends soldered to screws but derailments were extremely rare.

TOP
J
K
C
K
D
L
E
B
H
Fig 3
I
A
I
G
F

Fig 4
Pulley
Cord
Stop
Retracting bracket on door
Bottle

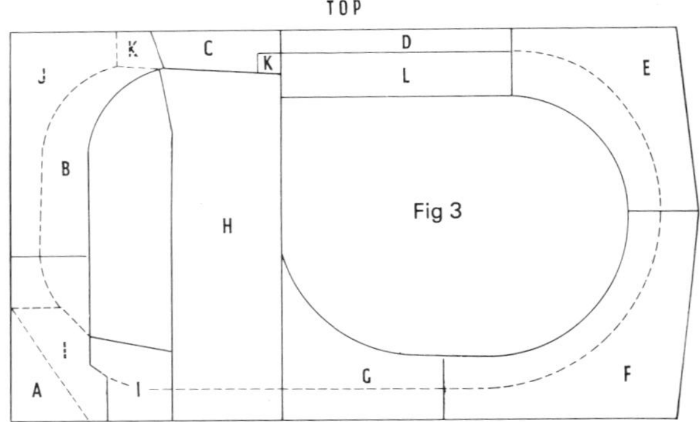

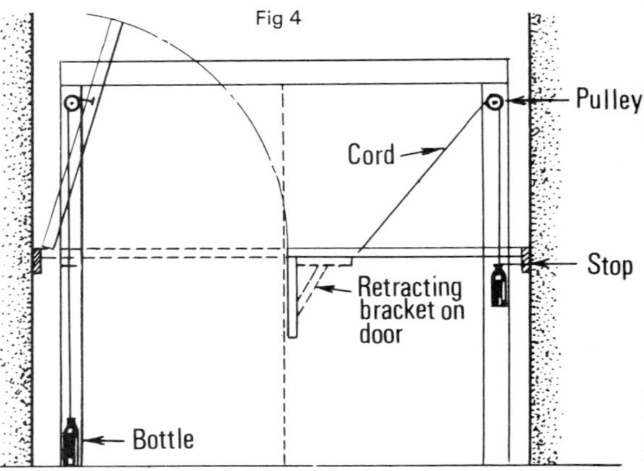

Above: *Looking down the platform at Victoria*

Track

The track and pointwork from a previous layout was salvaged with the addition of some extra points and yards of track brought the 'mileage' up to about 300ft, the actual route distance for a return journey being two scale miles. Various types of plain track had been used, but for the latest pointwork, in the recently rebuilt Victoria, 1/32in printed circuit board was used with good results. All the points but one were straightforward turnouts: there was no call for diamonds, slips, or other fancy items — except for one three-way point at Victoria — simplicity generally pays.

The track was laid on 3/32in roughened cork, which was a useful thickness for chamfering, looked well, and deadened the sound to just the right extent. The cork strips were stuck to the baseboard at their edges only, thus further adding to their cushioning properties — as well as saving glue! The track was for the most part floating, being anchored only at points and at the ends of the various boards. Elsewhere it was free to 'give' under traffic, but was held to alignment wherever necessary to maintain clearances or to prevent flexible straight sections from moving out of line under expansion. Short fishplates were used at rail joints within the length of an individual baseboard, and the rails were bonded throughout to minimise voltage drop.

Although harsh reverberation was eliminated, sufficient rail noise remained to combat the unrealistic sound of motors, while permitting the clickety-clicks to be authentically heard, and allow scale speed to be judged very accurately. Noise-producing joints were placed at around 4ft intervals, so that the front end of an average-length train picked up the next joint just after the rear had left the previous one behind.

Power Supply

The traction current was provided by four units working on individual supply. Those at Victoria and Clapham, largely used for shunting, were Codar modules, but the other two, for Croydon and the down main, were straight 100ohm rheostats. All four controllers had separate reversing switches, so that the 2in knobs had a conveniently large sweep of movement for easy and accurate control. Three of the units were fed from 16V, 1 amp. transformers, but the fourth transformer, with an output of 6 amps in 3V

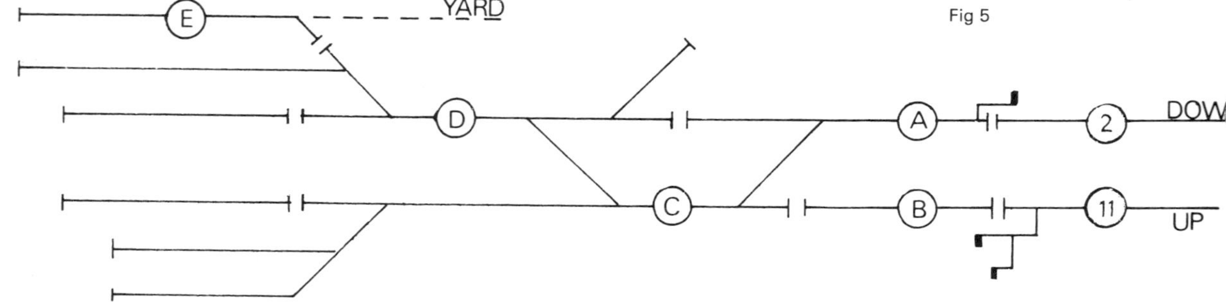

steps to 24V, also fed the relay, clock and lighting circuits. All the transformers and rectifiers were housed in a single transportable power-pack, from which multi-way cables took the current to the four control points on the baseboard edge.

Current Distribution

To build a layout is one thing, but to devise the most suitable control system is quite another, needing imagination and a lot of thought — especially with regard to visibility of stations and signals, and the varying numbers and ability of operators. The centralised, radial form of cab control (by which a train is driven from the same controller for the whole of its start-to-stop run), has some practical shortcomings so a special adaptation called Linked-Section control was used. In this, the main-line electrical sections were identical with the signalling sections (fig 1), and instead of being fed from the conventional battery of switches they were linked to each other, and to the appropriate controllers, by switches worked by the signal levers. In addition, within Victoria itself the current was fed from the correct controller to each platform, siding or spur merely by setting up and signalling the required route. This system was termed Signal-box Subsectioning. On the whole layout there were only three purely section switches: two of these were Yaxleys feeding the platform and shed dead-ends at Victoria, while the third was for the yard at Clapham — and was itself controlled by an interlocking lever in the signal-box.

In practice, the route was set up in response to the usual bell code messages from box to box along the line, and the current was automatically fed to each section involved from the controller that started the train on its run. This could be all the way down the line (or up), or between any other two stopping points, including the loop. On approaching a clear signal the driver knew the signalman was expecting him; that the line was clear; that the interlocked points were correctly set for the route, and that the track section ahead was switched to his own controller. As with the prototype, the driver drove on the signals, which went a long way towards capturing the real railway atmosphere.

Articles on these systems appeared in the model railway press during the '50s, but others may like to know a bit more about how they work. At Victoria (fig 5) the station was divided into six principal sub-sections, A to F. Section A was fed via a switch worked by the advanced starter lever: when this signal was 'on' the section was connected to the local Shunt controller, but when it was 'off' the section was linked to the Down Main controller, for departing trains. Sections C, D and E could be linked to A by switches worked via the three crossover levers, so that the Down Main current was fed to whatever part of the station the train was leaving from. Platforms 1, 4 and 5 were isolated by the points, but platforms 2 and 3, on 'normal' routes, were isolated through switches worked by the respective starter or inner home levers. All the signals were interlocked with the points, so that one could not get a clear signal unless the route was correctly set — and the current too.

For up trains, Section B (also normally connected to the Shunt controller) was linked to the up main feed rail instead, whenever the outer home signal was pulled off, Sections C, D and E being similarly linked to B, depending on the route set up for the arriving train. Thus the driver, who could be at either Clapham or Croydon, could take his train right up to the buffers, when the outer home signal was restored and the train given 'out of section'. Non-conflicting arrivals and departures could be routed simultaneously — while generally leaving the back of the station still available to the Shunt controller for loco and stock movements.

On the main line the analogous Linked-Section Control applied. Fig 6 shows the basic set-up at Clapham, for example. If the Clapham down home signal (DH) was clear, as at (a), then the down platform track (Section 3) was linked to Section 2 preceding the signal, so the Down Main driver could run a train right into the station. When the signal was restored, as at (b), the link was broken and the train was isolated. Having got 'line clear' from Croydon, the Clapham operator pulled off his starter (DS), as at (c), and thereby connected not only the platform track but also the block section ahead (Section 4) to his own controller. He could then drive the train on and restore the starter behind it, the block section still remaining on his controller, as at (d). At this point his home signal could be pulled off for the next down train, so that very close working was achieved when necessary. Similar switchgear existed at Croydon, a clear signal allowing the Clapham driver to take the train into either of the down platform roads, the splitting signal showed for which road the points were set.

For through trains Clapham would get 'line clear' from Croydon as soon as possible and then pull off both his down home *and* his down starter, as at (e). The effect of this was to link Sections 3 *and* 4 back to Section 2, Croydon's down home again linking Section 5 to Section 4. For an express, Croydon would pull off his own starter as well, linking the loop (Section 6) back to Section 5, and so on, thus allowing the Down Main driver to proceed non-stop all the way. But you had to keep signals 'off' at intermediate stations until a through train finished its run or you cut it off in its prime. (Through freights from Clapham to Reigate were handled in the same way.)

The same circuitry existed on the up line too, so while Clapham was passing a fast train through in one direction his own controller was free either to drive another train in the opposite direction, or to carry on shunting the yard. For main line shunting movements the platform roads were fed through switches worked by the associated points, while the yard, as stated earlier, was on a separate circuit.

Wherever some form of Cab Control is practical, Linked-Section Control does have several advantages over the conventional switch-board system, thus:

It is simpler (only one group of controls to deal with); it is safer (no conflict between route and current, also over-running a signal stops a train); more realistic (signals give continuous indication of road (and

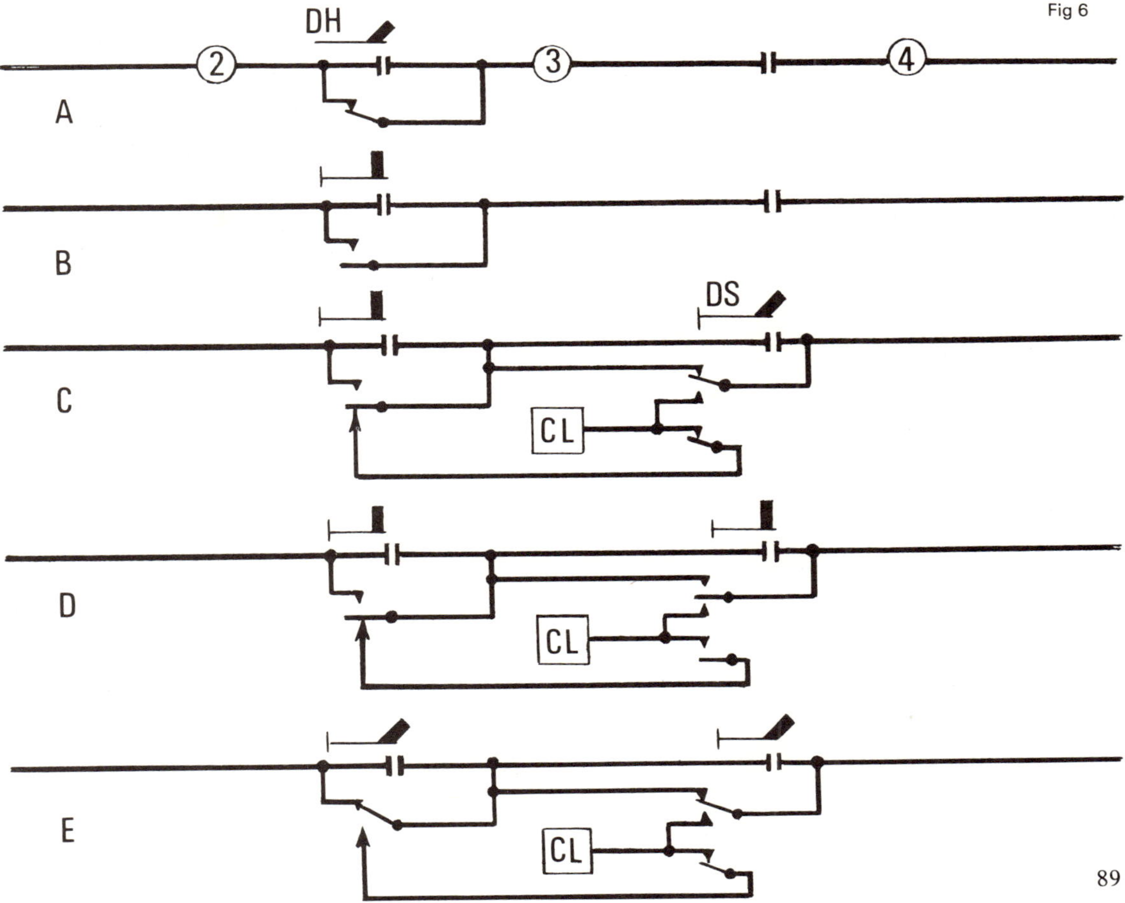

current) to both signalman and driver); more convenient and flexible (no need for any overall centralised control); neater and more compact (controls are less out of scale and can go in normal size signal-box); and cheaper (home-made switchgear, no inter-station wiring, no elaborate switchboard).

Return Loop

Compared with the normal fiddle yard, a concealed return loop maintains far more convincingly the illusion of 'romantic places' far afield — especially if it has more than one track, so that the last train down is never the first train back, and even more so if it works automatically. For then, when a train runs 'off the map' it is not only out of sight but also, out of mind: no one, can recall what trains are hibernating in the tunnel, waiting to reappear at the scheduled time. And since what had been a down Tunbridge Wells was liable to emerge, considerably later, as an up East Grinstead, and since in the meantime the Croydon operator had to make other movements, the illusion that a train really had been where it was due to go was nearly complete.

By contrast, a fiddle yard — even if hidden from public view — can never deceive the owner or his fellow operators: it can be all right for exhibitions, but falls down badly as an attempt at private illusion.

On this layout the return loop was equivalent to the section in advance on the down line and the section in rear on the up line. The Croydon switch-gear followed the same principle as that at Clapham, but was somewhat modified for the loop. The latter was normally dead, but could be linked to the down line when the down starter was off, and to the up line when the up home was off. To avoid confusion the home signal could not take effect except on the up platform track so long as the starter was off. This did not prevent an up train being brought out of Reigate on the Croydon controller while a down train was being driven to the loop by Clapham or Victoria. The loop was, as usual, fed from Croydon through the same rheostat as the main line, but via a separate reversing switch (normally set for clockwise travel).

The Passing Loop

On entering the return loop tunnel a train would run into whichever of the two hidden roads was vacant. As it did so it actuated two ramps that completed a relay circuit which reversed the points, stopped the train, and switched the current to the other road. Thus, when the next up train was due and Croydon reversed his controller and pulled off his up home signal, he would bring out not the last down train but the one before it.

The ramps were wheel-actuated, so it did not matter which way round an emu set was running. The first ramp on each road was placed just after the Y-points, and fired a holding relay which also partly set up the point motor circuit. The second ramp was reached by the front of the longest train just after the rear had passed the first ramp, and its action was to complete the trailing point motor circuit via the holding relay. As the trailing point motor fired, it transferred the current to the facing point and at the same time released the holding circuit on the down starter, thus stopping the train. As the facing point motor fired it cut off its own current by breaking down the holding circuit initially set up for that road. This ensured that only the *next* down train could change the points again. There was a similar circuit for the other track. Normally the whole thing looked after itself, but a manual over-ride was provided by a Yaxley switch worked by a lever in the Reigate box. This allowed one to select either road at will, or else to cut the changeover out altogether for testing purposes.

The Branch

Reigate (section 7, fig 1) drew its current automatically from either the down side of the loop (Section 6) or from the up main (Section 8), depending on whether the junction was set for a down or an up local. For shunting, the up route-setting lever at Reigate was pulled off half-way — thus reversing the junction and feeding the power to Reigate, but not clearing the Reigate starting signal even though the up main signal was put to danger mechanically by the point motor relay. In this half-way position, too, a switch worked by the lever cut out one half of the DC traction supply and put Reigate on pulse power. This was quite helpful with some locos when you wanted to creep up to an uncoupler. When the lever was either normal or fully reversed, full-wave rectification was restored.

For down trains into Reigate the main line junction signal was put to danger mechanically when the points were reversed, but the branch signal came off, electrically, only when the lever movement was completed, thus avoiding the odd sight of two semaphores moving in opposite ways at once. The Reigate up starter cleared in the same way when the lever movement was completed.

Other Refinements

There were several subsidiary circuits, including automatic distants, a 'train-on-line' warning light for the loop, and a couple of extra interlocks on the Croydon box to prevent false moves. With the point/signal interlocking as well, the unseen switchgear was fairly extensive, yet it was simple circuitry.

The Scenic Side

As can be seen from the plan of the baseboards, there were openings in the middle of the layout — necessary to accommodate the car and of course, the operators.

Above: *A view of Reigate Junction showing the return tunnel.* / P. J. Kelly

The scenery was effective yet kept to the minimum. There were no vast built-up areas full of super detail, yet it was assumed it was there. The station buildings at Croydon, Clapham and Reigate were handbuilt, yet again were not super detailed but quite effective. Victoria did not have an overall roof as this would have got in the way of operation and made it difficult for a driver to bring his train to within ½in of the buffers.

Apart from the Clapham goods shed which was the familiar Superquick model, although suitably dirtied, the other major building was the loco shed at Victoria which was a Peter Denny cast-off. The signal boxes, which had proper lever frames, consisted of a handbuilt one in the style of the prototype for Reigate; an improved Superquick with the characteristic overhang of the Old North box at Croydon; while Clapham was a scratch-built modern affair standing between the inner and outer levels.

The chalk cuttings were made from Polyfilla mixed with dirt and cork filings from the track underlays where they had been chamfered, the whole lot plastered on to a hardboard backing. Grass was old carpet felt painted with green Temera colour, and where the brown showed through on the odd spots it added to the realism.

Signals

Generally the signals were of the semaphore type, despite the fact that the system represented the SR in the '50s. This was because many of them had to be read from behind as well as from the front. Where

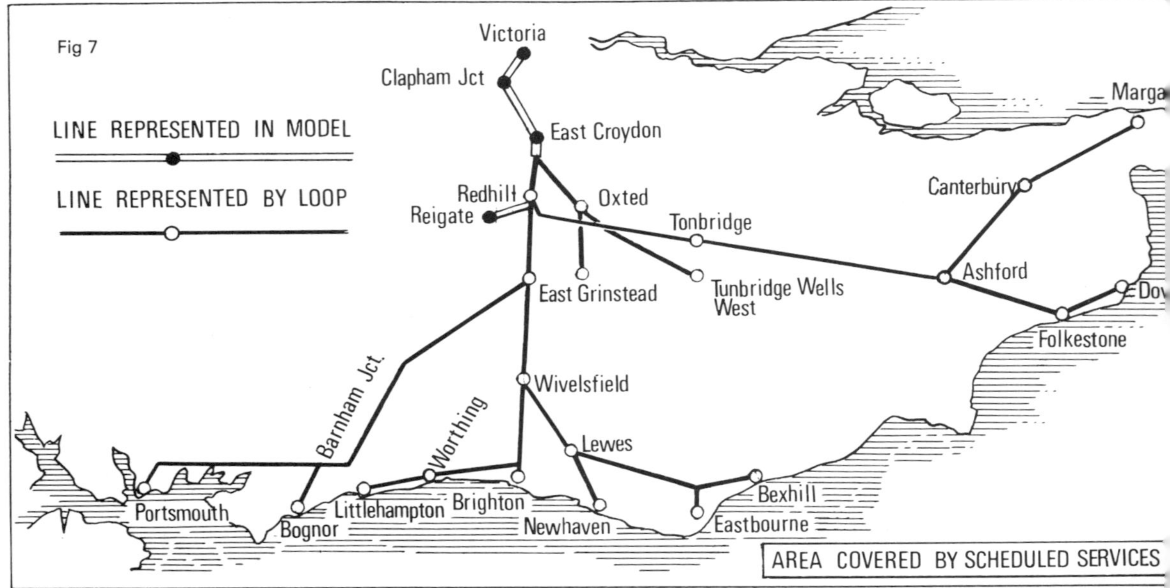

distant signals were included they were usually either fixed or worked in tandem with the starters above them. Those beneath the up Croydon and down Clapham starters were worked by an automatic slotting circuit, so they only came off when the local starter and the next two stop signals were clear, a useful indication for the driver of a fast non-stop train.

Rolling Stock

Being a SR layout representing the mid-50s, it was natural that electric multiple units should predominate the scene and the emu roster was:

Stock	*Destination*	*Type of Service*	*Headcode*
5 BEL	Brighton	Express	4
6 PUL	Brighton	Semi-fast	6
6 PUL	Littlehampton	Semi-fast	16
4 COR	Portsmouth	Semi-fast	26
4 COR	Eastbourne	Semi-fast	52
2 BIL	Brighton	Slow	14
2 BIL	Reigate	Slow	34

To balance things up steam hauled trains worked services from South Croydon to East Grinstead and Tunbridge Wells, plus those from Redhill to Ashford and points east, not to mention the Newhaven line, as shown in Fig 7. These were served by a 3 coach 60ft birdcage set, with first-class saloon; a four-coach Hastings set, and a BR type boat train with utility van. There were also freight and parcels traffic, some of which originated at Clapham.

The loco stud, all with scale back-to-back wheels was as follows:

Hornby-Dublo West Country.
Hornby 2-8-0 Class 8F.
Hornby 2-6-4T.
Hornby 0-6-0T Class R1.

Tri-ang 4-4-0 Class L1.
Tri-ang Co-Co Diesel.
(spare).

Co-Co electric No 20002.
2-6-0 U Class built from a Wills kit.

Models were only hand-built if they could not be purchased, so most of the coaching stock was hand-built.

Basically, wood was used for coach roofs, floors and ends, with each of the sides made of a single strip of 1/16in Perspex, filed to a curve below the waistline where necessary. A shellacked card overlay (with the windows and door drop-lights cut out by means of a celluloid jig for locating the straight-edge) was stuck on to the Perspex with a non-active and damp-resistant mixture of Cow gum and black Bostik. This construction gave a good weight of coach which stood up to years of handling, running, and climatic changes. Most of the coaches dated from 1957 or earlier, yet despite numerous mishaps they looked pretty good 15 years later. The automatic couplings were non-magnetic hook-and-bar developed from the Walkley on the lines later adopted by Tri-ang, but within each rake of coaches I use a special spring-clip type (fig 8). This was especially convenient beneath corridor connections, as one had only to line up the pivoting end and push the vehicles together — a godsend in the tunnel!

Above: *East Croydon station, with an East Grinstead train departing behind a Hornby Dublo 2-6-4T, while a Reigate bound emu waits on the down relief to follow as soon as the section is clear. A steam hauled up train is on the nearest platform. The line above carries an up Portsmouth 4-COR unit to Victoria* / P. J. Kelly

The Service

It is obvious that neither an end-to-end nor a continuous-run type of layout would enable all these trains to be operated realistically, which was one reason why a return loop was decided on. After reaching a point somewhere south of Croydon all trains except those for Reigate disappeared off the map — to reappear quite a bit later on the up line on their return journey. (Fig 9, showing diagrammatically the electrical sections and signals, as well as the route and general arrangement, will recall the scale plan and schematic diagram of the line). This arrangement not only provided a large number of theoretical destinations for the trains, but also saved the operators running round them and fetching them back again. An

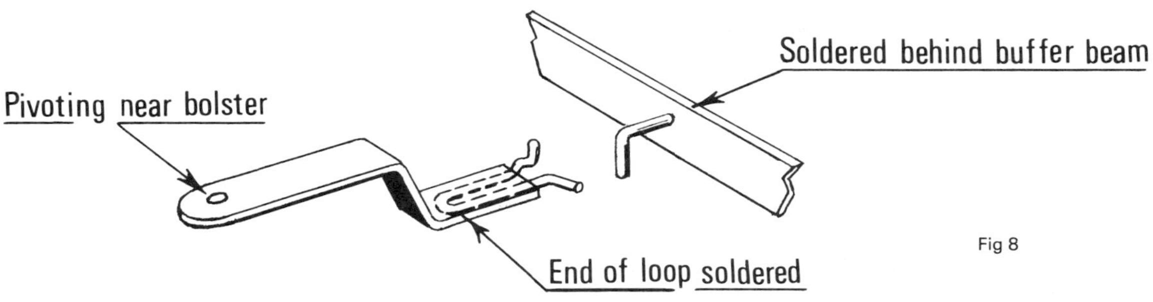

Fig 8

Fig 9

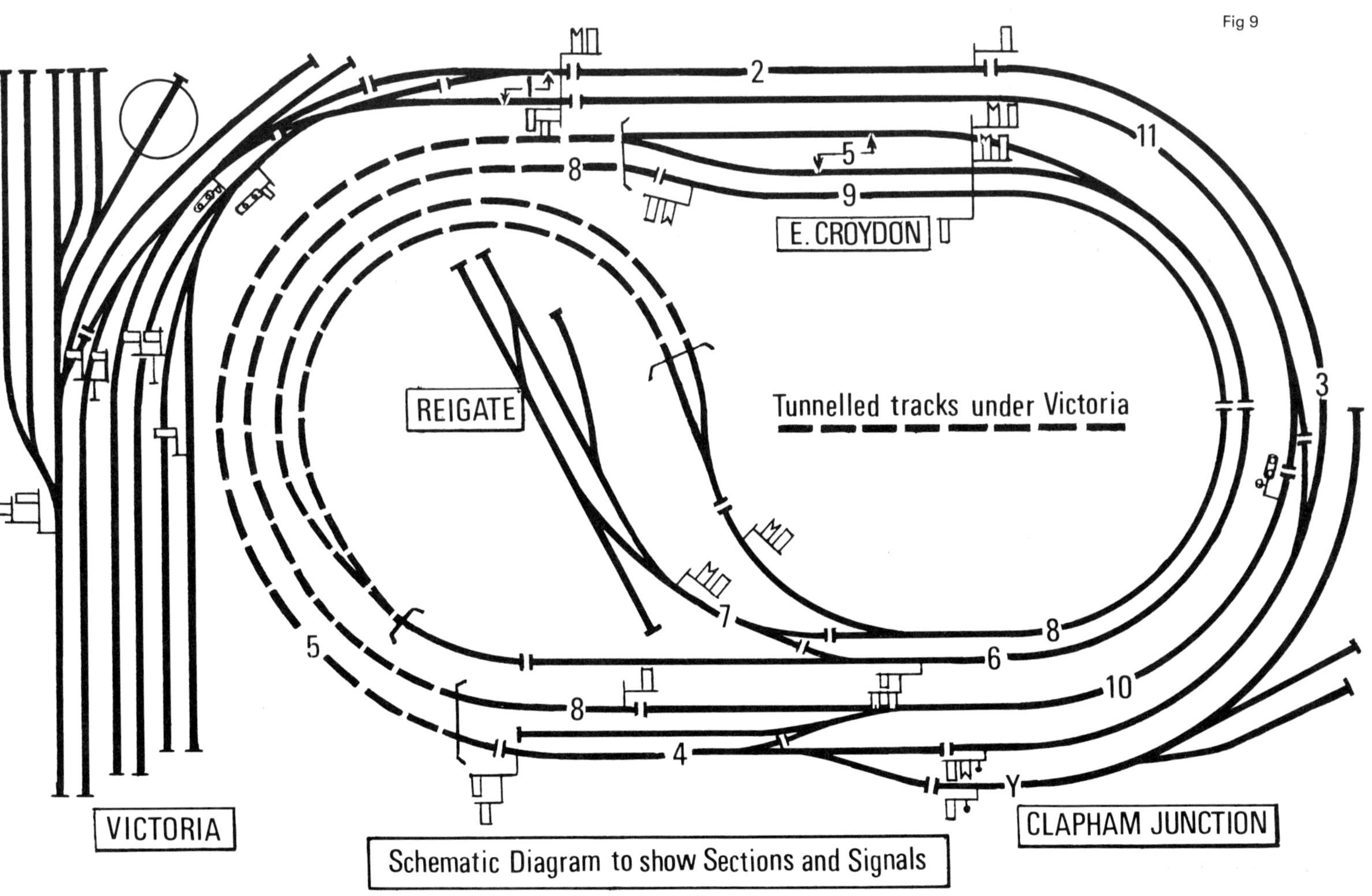

Schematic Diagram to show Sections and Signals

incidental advantage of the return loop was that trains got reversed *en route,* and thus faced the opposite way on alternate journeys. Hence, by fitting different head-codes at opposite ends one could correctly route the 6 PUL to Brighton and Littlehampton in turn, while the 4 COR similarly alternated between Portsmouth and Eastbourne.

The various trains served theoretical destinations from Margate round to Portsmouth, as well as Reigate, Tunbridge Wells and East Grinstead, and the railway was run to a repeating eight-hour schedule.

The full schedule was made up of two four-hour periods, at the end of each the hinging sections were conveniently free of stock.

Preparing the Schedule

Working out a new schedule was quite a long and tricky — though fascinating — business. Experience had shown that the line worked best if there were about five down and five up trains in each time-table hour — plus odd light engine and empty stock runs between Clapham and Victoria. The first thing was to draft a likely-looking pattern of possible departures, based on the 1956 time-table and on the locos and rolling stock available. During the eight hour period each train, including freight and parcels, would make four to six journeys, using different locos where possible in order to add variety, and for each destination there was only a limited number of prototype departure times available. After some preliminary juggling one started on a tentative time and motion graph, of which fig 10 shows just one hour, and then gradually adjusted and refined it until the best possible balance had been achieved. Requirements were:

1 to get a varied sequence of trains.
2 to arrange for platform and siding accommodation.
3 to roster different yet suitable locos on successive runs.
4 to make sure that locos don't block each other on shed.
5 to check that no driver was scheduled to drive two trains at the same time in opposite directions.
6 to keep something happening almost continuously on the main line.
7 to avoid scheduling a train to emerge from the return loop while it was still sitting on the dead track.
8 to use the Croydon relief road and Clapham lay-by siding to change the order of trains.
9 to provide interesting shunts at Clapham and Reigate.
10 to work in the occasional simultaneous arrival and departure at Victoria.

Quite a job . . . and it was essential to have a platform and siding occupation chart for each hour below the corresponding graph, so that a constant check can be made of what was practicable.

How these various factors were reconciled may be seen by studying fig 10. It represents return journeys via Reigate or either of the return loop tracks during the hour from 11.00 to 11.59. One time-table minute per block section was allowed, and this — with ample recovery time at intermediate stations — permit leisurely acceleration, unhurried cruising, and gentle

Below: *A general view of Clapham yard and station.*

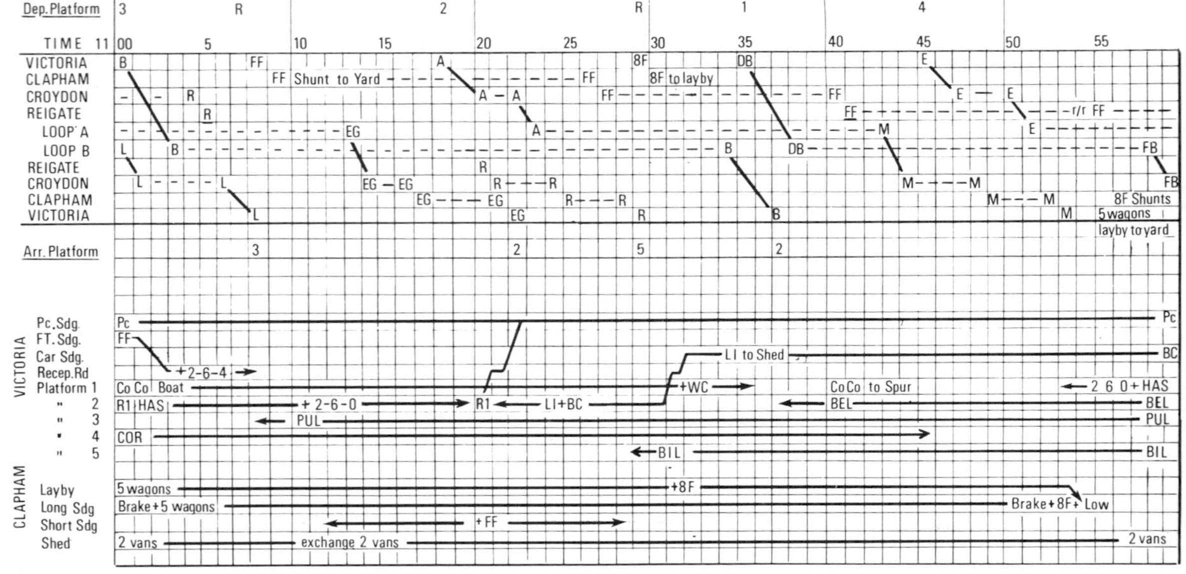

Fig 10

		E	*Eastbourne*
		FB	*Folkestone Boat train*
B	*Brighton Belle*	*Pc*	*Parcels*
R	*Reigate*	*BC*	*Birdcage set*
L	*Littlehampton*	*HAS*	*Hastings set*
FF	*Fitted Freight*	*W/C*	*West Country*
EG	*East Grinstead*	*Fr*	*Freight*
A	*Ashford*	*Car*	*Carriage*
DB	*Dover Boat train*	*Sdg*	*Siding*
M	*Margate*	*Recep*	*Reception road*

stops. At the left, the 10.48 Reigate train waits on Croydon down relief road for the 11.00 Brighton Belle to run through to the loop, to occupy the track just vacated by the up Littlehampton, now standing in Croydon on the up main. As soon as the Belle has finished its run, Croydon is free to drive the Reigate train to Reigate (arr 11.05) and then take the up Littlehampton non-stop to Victoria (dep 11.06). As this train runs into Victoria at 11.08 the fitted freight makes a simultaneous departure, timed to allow Clapham to shunt it to the yard (for an exchange of vans) comfortably in advance of the departure of the 11.18 Ashford train. Meanwhile, at 11.13 Croydon pulls off his up home signal and brings the up East Grinstead out of the loop, stops it at Croydon, and then offers it on to Clapham for departure at 11.16. There it waits while the Ashford train runs through to Croydon, where the up Reigate arrives a minute later — waiting there while the Croydon operator drives the Ashford train to the loop (where it automatically takes the empty road left by the up East Grinstead). Meanwhile (again) the Clapham operator, having finished his shunt, is ready to take the East Grinstead on to Victoria, where it runs into Platform 2 — vacated four minutes earlier by the down Ashford train — see track occupation chart.

It will be seen that for the most part movements on the main line were made consecutive, so as to avoid dead spots, but here and there some overlaps did occur. At 11.34, for instance, the up Brighton Belle had to leave the loop *after* Clapham had finished shunting the 8F to the layby, but in time to leave a free road for the 11.35 down Dover train. Hence the two over-lapping non-stop runs. At the end of the hour Clapham again occupied both up and down lines for a shunt, but Croydon filled in the time by running round the fitted freight at Reigate.

Having got this graph seemingly right, the next step was to write out in pencil in plain language the departure and arrival schedule for Victoria, leaving hefty blanks for stock and loco shunting movements. These were then filled in by considering what moves would have to precede each departure and what sequence has to follow each South-Eastern arrival. A separate history of each loco's movements acts as a check on these calculations.

At this stage a single-handed dummy run, was operated using the pencilled schedule for Victoria and the graph for Croydon and Clapham.

Fig 11 actually shows Croydon's duties for the hour covered by Fig 10. The train descriptions imply *down* trains unless otherwise stated, and the levers required are shown on the right. This enabled a newcomer to get on with the job with very little preliminary briefing. Levers in Croydon box were shown in red, and those in Reigate box (which he also handled) preceded by an R and shown in black. The Clapham schedule was on the same plan, but a separate shunting schedule was provided, with lettered cross-references to the main schedule. Magnetic place-markers were supplied for each schedule, and these were a great boon.

The Clock

An hour of schedule usually took around half-an-hour of real time — depending on how well the Clapham operator coped with his shunting. In order to cater for different levels of efficiency a variable-speed clock which could run at anything between normal speed and four times faster was used. This allowed extra time for learners when needed, or to keep things really humming when experts were on hand.

Operators

The normal operating team was four — one to each control point. Driving the down line was the easiest job, and was done from the most comfortable position, with the best all-round view of the layout. Sitting back in the corner by the Croydon down home signals, listening to the bell codes and watching the trains wend their way round the line, and occasionally driving a train to Clapham or Croydon, or all the way to the loop with the Brighton Belle or a boat train — was most relaxing and enjoyable.

The driver-signalman at Croydon had a fairly easy job, though he did have the odd Reigate run-round to attend to, but at Clapham a single-handed operator could have some quite hectic spells — especially when he was bombarded with through trains from both directions at once just as he was in the middle of a complicated shunt.

The line could be run — though less enjoyably — by three, or even two operators. In the latter case Clapham box was closed by the simple process of pulling off the four running signals and switching the Victoria bell through to Croydon and vice versa. For single-handed testing of trains or track Victoria had a remote series rheostat in the Croydon traction feed line, so one person could control both the down and the up lines throughout their length from the Victoria operating bay. Remote push-buttons to work the Croydon and Reigate point and signal relays also helped in single-handed running.

Fig 11

Time	*Action*	*Train Description*	*Levers*
11.00	Accept & pass	BRIGHTON BELLE EXP. to loop	1; 4
04	dispatch	REIGATE, relief to Reigate	3, 4/R1
06	Dispatch	up LITTLEHAMPTON Fast to Vic.	2
13	Bring on	up EAST GRINSTEAD (stops)	5
16	Dispatch	up EAST GRINSTEAD to Clapham	2
18	Accept	ASHFORD (stops)	1
20	Bring on	up REIGATE (stops)	5/R2
22	Dispatch	ASHFORD to loop	4
24	Dispatch	up REIGATE to Clapham	2
26	Accept	FITTED FREIGHT to relief	3, 1
34	Bring on & pass	up BRIGHTON BELLE EXP. to Vic.	5; 2
35	Accept & pass	DOVER BOAT EXPRESS to loop	1; 4
40	Dispatch	FITTED FREIGHT to Reigate	3, 4/R4, 1
43	Bring on	up MARGATE (stops)	5
45	Accept	EASTBOURNE (stops)	1
48	Dispatch	up MARGATE to Clapham	2
50	Dispatch	EASTBOURNE to loop	4
52	Run round	FITTED FREIGHT at Reigate	R2 plus 4/6
58	Bring on	up FOLKESTONE BOAT (stops)	5

NB. ; means pull following lever only when line clear ahead
R precedes Reigate levers.

Below: *A down Newhaven Boat Train entering East Croydon down main platform. On the extreme left of the photograph can be seen the tunnel from Reigate.*

A 7mm scale LNER Branch Line in the Garden

Photographs by
BRIAN MONAGHAN

Right: *The terminus of the branch line is Bunker Bay station and here waiting to leave are LNER Class C1 4-4-2 and Class D10 4-4-0 with trains and a streamlined Class A4* Wild Swan *waits the road for a light engine.*

Below: *One of the joys of a garden railway in the summer. Here an LNER Class J69 0-6-0 No 2974 is at the head of a mixed parcels van train in ideal surroundings.*

Left: *Near Glasshouse Junction the line runs alongside real plants and shrubs and here a Class P2 2-8-2 No 2001* Cock o' the North *and Class A4 4-6-4 No 4467* Wild Swan *pass each other.*

Above: *An old timer in the shape of Stirling designed GNR No 1 approaches the main terminal station.*

BUNKER
6430
L N E R
46202

Left: *Another view of Bunker Bay station with Class D10 4-4-0 No 5430* Purdon Viccars *attracting some admirers on the platform. The LMSR is allowed to run over the line and their Turbomotive rebuilt as No 45202* Princess Anne *is in the foreground.*

Top: Cock o' the North *comes round the shrubbery.*

Above: *A busy scene as an LMSR sleeping car express passes on the main line and an LNER local train is on the left. A goods train is fronted by an ex-CR 0-6-0 No 17652.*

L N E R
1879
L N E R
8297
1698
L N E R
MODEL
RAILWAY ENGINEERS
R.F. STEDMAN & Co. Ltd
HUNSLET, LEEDS
36
N E
E 507077
L M S
L M S
L M S
N E
N
12 TONS
M S
S

Left: *Looking across the goods yard to the main platforms at Bunker Bay station.*

Above: *An LNER express sweeps round a gentle bend and over a small bridge. Features realistically employed in this garden railway.*

Right: *A neat 7mm scale cross-over in the station platforms.*

The Best of Both Worlds

ANTHONY RALLS

A short article entitled 'Why Go Continental?' appeared in the January 1969 issue of *Model Railway Constructor,* in which Roger Pound made some very good points on the interest and advantages of modelling continental railways, with especial reference to the SNCF. If this article received as much attention as it deserved there is no need to re-iterate its arguments.

Some years ago, when we moved into a top-floor flat, I was allocated, by family democratic processes, a cupboard 5ft 6in by 4ft 10in leading out of a corner of the living-room, into which I could put the railway. (It was mentioned, as an aside, that any normal person would have turned it into a bar, but . . .) A sort of spiral layout was begun, which was to be a fictitious branch of the Somerset & Dorset Joint Railway. This line was to connect the S&DJR main line north of Sturminster Newton with the GW Westbury-Salisbury line just east of Warminster. It would climb through Mere and Zeals to a summit near Stourhead (lots of excursion traffic) and then run down the valley of the Wylye. By one of those vagaries of parliamentary decisions, it was decreed that the Somerset & Dorset could only own the line as far as the Wiltshire border — the part within the county of Wilts must be Great Western. This thoroughly impracticable way of running a railway, especially one that would provide the quickest route of all between South Wales and Bournemouth, persuaded the GWR to do a deal with its inveterate enemy the S&DJR so the whole branch became operated as a joint line.

Thus the layout grew up. The cupboard, of course could only contain a section of the branch. A portable extension, shaped to fit in the window-bay of the living-room, joins on to the permanent layout through the doorway of the cupboard. This extension carries a station with three platform faces, a central lay-by line and a siding; also a banjo-loop which is very useful for getting whole trains to face the other way, or for turning tender-locomotives. The track is an assortment of Hornby Dublo, Peco, and Playcraft-Jouef, with one double-slip by Fleischmann. The ruling gradient is about 1 in 40 (according to my amateur survey, that on the prototype, if it existed, would be about 1 in 60). Most of the civil engineering and architectural works are home-made, but include a certain amount of Airfix and Hambling-Merco kits cannibalised as necessary, and residences and shops are (West German) manufactured kits adapted. Signalling, it must be admitted, has always been rudimentary, but this will be referred to again later.

Rolling-stock is from many sources: hand-built with or without Merco printed sides; Airfix and Kenline kits; second-hand Dublo and Tri-ang vehicles either re-built or just re-painted. Through passenger trains are of GWR or S&DJR and Midland stock, hauled by a Castle or a S&DJR Class 2P assisted if necessary by a Class 3F. Local traffic may be a GWR saddle-tank with a push-pull trailer, or a LSWR Class G6 tank with a couple of non-corridor coaches. Freight traffic finds itself being hustled around by a S&DJR 2-8-0 or Class 3F, or a Collett Goods, and on occasions is startled by a powerful heave from GWR No 40 (ex-Rhymney No 44 0-6-2T) sent down by Swindon on a running-in turn.

The timetable was based on existing trains at Warminster and Sturminster Newton in the timetables for I forget which year, and through traffic does in fact fit in quite neatly.

That was It — until a friend persuaded me to set my alarm for 3am one Sunday in May 1966, drive 120 miles to London, and go on the LCGB trip to France. I drove back from London between 12 and 3 on the Monday morning in a rosy daze, having fallen, hook line and sinker, for the SNCF.

During the next few weeks I begged, borrowed and scrounged any literature I could trace on the French Railways — its history, its locomotives, their performances, and so on. Telling myself that I only wanted them to Gaze At and Daydream, I acquired a A3B5myfi coach and a postal van by Jouef. Gazing at them, I began to realise how 'narrow-gauge and top-heavy' my OO stock looked in comparison with HO. (It also dawned on me that these were so cheap that it wouldn't be worth the time it would take to build anything comparable. It also appeared that their rolling qualities were such that they got under way if you sneezed behind them.) Day-dreaming I estimated that a seven-coach train in HO might be shorter than a six-coach train in OO.

Well, it was obvious. Some motive power, other than sneezing, was needed. The cheapest and easiest to get hold of, which would make a reasonable beginning, was the standard Jouef Pacific. Thanks to the prices and the varied range of Jouef rolling-stock, there were

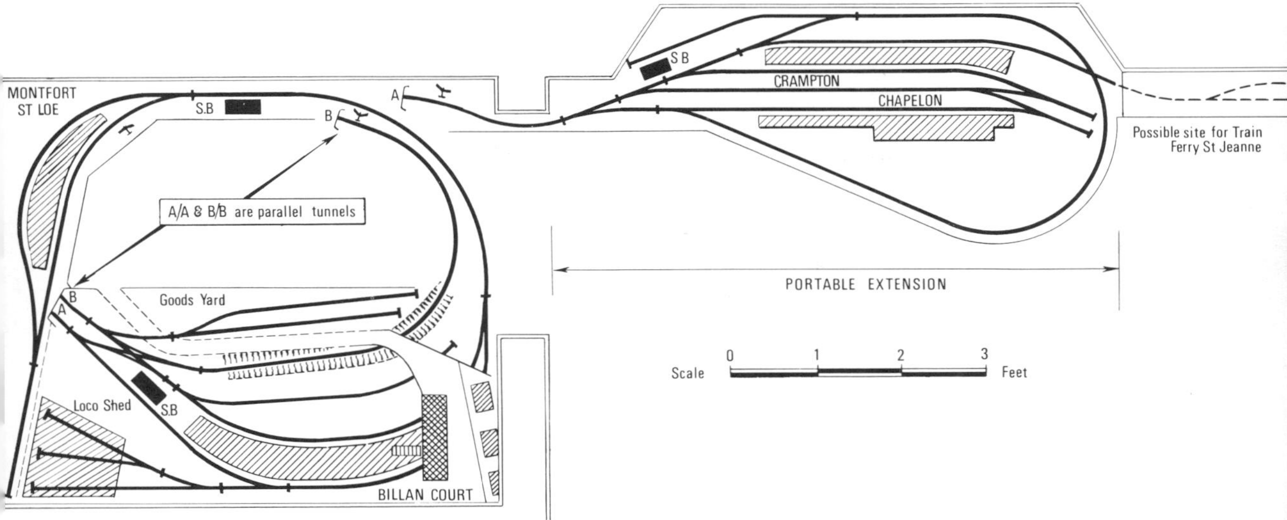

Below: *SDJR No 44 4-4-0 in Montfort St Loe station.*

"... not to stand too close to the edge of the platform..."

soon more vehicles than the Pacific could tackle, so more locomotives were needed. French steam-outline models are nothing like so cheap as the stuff they haul, so scratch-building was called for. In two years I managed to produce 050TD167 — one of those huge ten-coupled tanks one sees shifting empty stock around Calais and Boulogne — and 231E22, the beautiful Chapelon Pacific which had captivated me on that Sunday in 1966. I also went quite crackers and bought a Jouef Autorail Panoramique — one of the 10 glamorous double-deck railcars — which my friends call the 'unknown flying object'. Apparently if there is to be a trailer for this, I shall have to build it. Jouef produce one (Ref 851) but no one this side of the Channel wants to know about it. Further additions to the rolling-stock were three bargain Hornby Acho coaches, and three beautiful Lima vehicles which came as Christmas presents. With the Lima's you don't even have to sneeze; in fact if you want them to stay put, you have to hold your breath, and they can only be parked on a dead level siding. By contrast, the Achos are heavy and take some pulling.

So, now there are two complete sets of stock: the 4mm collection of GWR and S&DJR and the 3.5mm SNCF collection. I can have the best — well, perhaps the next best, because of the unavoidable compromises — of both worlds. There is a chest of drawers under part of the layout, and when I get the urge to cross the Channel, the English lot goes into one drawer, and the French lot comes out of another. All the wretched motorists on the roads have to start driving on the right; all the little people suddenly find themselves 87/76ths taller (even the girl in the topless dress chatting with a policeman who suddenly turns into a gendarme as tall as Mon Général) and the Café Maigret across the road from Billan Court station finds itself released from licensing hours and can sell cognac at a reasonable price. By the way, the station names are neutral: 'Montfort St Loe' could equally well be in Somerset or Calvados.

But there have to be compromises. I can almost feel the shudders of the purists over much that has already been told! The scenery and civil engineering is no real worry: after all, it must be admitted, the majority of structures on OO layouts are on the small side, because space demands it; so they look better rather than worse, with HO scale trains. But station platforms and signals are real problems. The compromise over station platforms, of having them low by English standards and rather high for France, has a practical advantage that I do not recall having seen mentioned elsewhere: platforms on curves can follow the line of the track more exactly and realistically as the overhang of long vehicles passes over the platform edge instead of fouling it. (The little people have to be trained not to stand too close to the

Top left: *SDJR No 81 2-8-0 and a MR brake van in Montfort St Loe station.*

Centre left: *Crampton-Chapelon station with 231E22 4-6-2 at head of train and a Autorail Panoramique (Jouef model) in station platform. The ten-coupled tank is nearest camera.*

Below: *The ex-Nord 050TD167 loco.*

edge — a visit to the chiropodist for treatment with UHU is good for giving them a sense of responsibility in this matter!)

That leaves the problem of signals. It has already been mentioned that signals on this layout have always been rudimentary, and even that state has deteriorated over the years. The variety of signals in use on the SNCF is quite fascinating, but I do not yet know anything like enough about them to tackle the job thoroughly. The best solution, probably, will be to have 'plug-in' signal-posts with French or English signals which can replace each other as required, and be operated from the same controls. As and when this solution is achieved, it might form the subject of a separate account.

Brief details of the locomotives may be of interest. Beginning this side of the Channel:

S&DJR No 44 (2P 4-4-0) An old Tri-ang L1 with altered cab-sides, chimney, bogie, and various additional details. The tender is from a 3F.

S&DJR No 72 (3F 2-8-0) A Tri-ang 3F, with a more scale chimney and detail alterations.

S&DJR No 81 (7F 2-8-0) The chassis is that of a Hornby Dublo Stanier Class 8F with Ringfield motor. The cylinder assembly has been tilted. From the footplate up it is hand-built, slightly over scale length because of the length of the chassis. The tender is of the original type with a half-cab; this was essential to hide the huge motor which projects into, and almost fills, the cab of the loco.

Those three locomotives are in S&D blue livery with gold lettering and numbers.

GWR No 5070 *Sir Daniel Gooch* A Hornby Dublo Castle bought second-hand for £2 and in need of no attention whatever beyond touching up the paint work. Fairly powerful and beautifully smooth running.

GWR No 2204 (Collett 0-6-0) The chassis is a Dublo 0-6-0. The boiler and parts of the tender are from an Airfix Truro kit, The remainder was cooked up from odds and ends.

GWR No 2012 (Dean) 0-6-0ST A Hornby Tri-ang 0-6-0 chassis, back to front, to leave the open cab free of projections such as the motor. Scratch-built from processed-pea tins and Plastikard, with commercial chimney and dome. Painted lake-colour, 1909 style.

GWR No 40 (ex-Rhymney Rly No 44 0-6-2T) A Hornby Dublo 0-6-2T, considerably butchered. Sand-boxes removed; new chimney; Belpaire fire-box and boiler top-feed added. Result, a fairly accurate model of No 40 in the period between being taken over and being re-boilered by Swindon.

LSWR No 277 (G6 0-6-0T) Originally (many years ago) a Tri-ang 'Jinty'. The Belpaire fire-box was removed, and the cab re-built. Stove-pipe chimney, correct safety valves, and sand-boxes added. Apple-green livery, lettered LSWR in gold; oval number plates with red background.

It will have been noticed that the foregoing do not all belong to the same period. They therefore do not appear all at once! One tries to avoid obvious anachronisms, but not to get too depressed if one fails! To continue on the other side of the water:

SNCF 231 C 60 Collin (Nord) Super-Pacific The standard Jouef Pacific, plus polished brass boiler-bands, ladders in front of the cylinders, 'cinéma' (train-

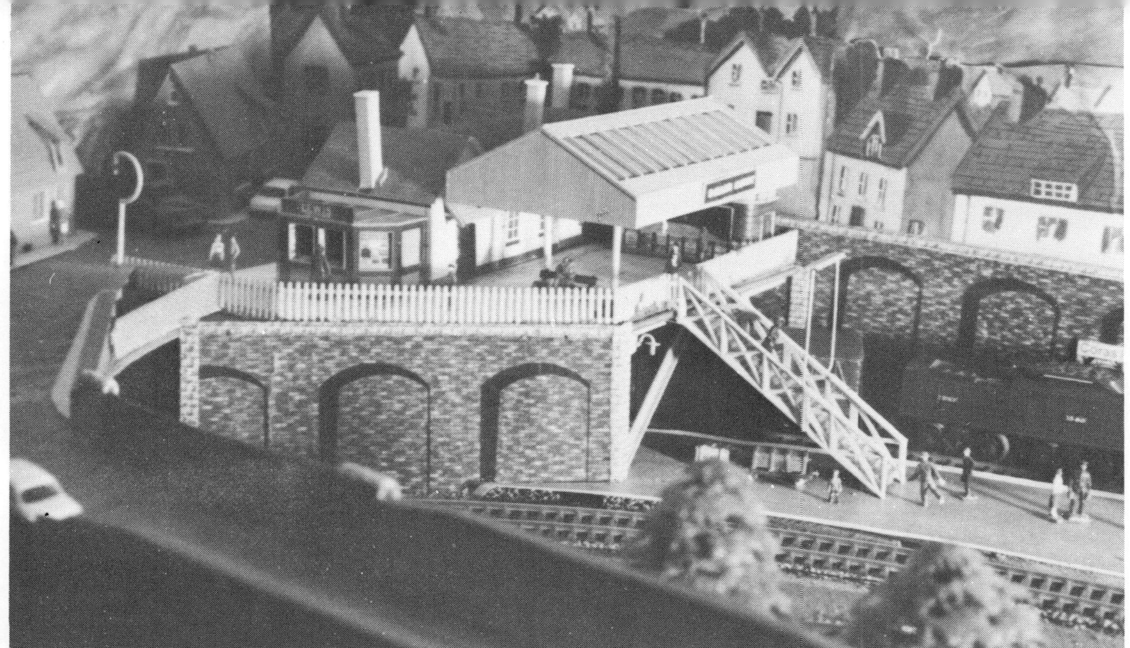

Above left: *The Crampton-Chapelon Pacific 231E22 loco.*

Above: *Billan Court station.*

number indicator) and additional head-light. Mechanically, this model is quite unlike any of the others. It has a huge motor driving through a crown-and-pinion and a train of gears; it therefore 'has no brakes' and will coast for a yard or two when the current is switched off. Runs on less than ¼amp, so a couple of lamp-bulbs have to be switched into the circuit to reduce the current and make it controllable (incidentally, these bulbs illuminate the loco shed). It is a masterpiece of efficient simplicity, but because of its unusual mechanism one has to 'learn to drive' it. Painted SNCF green.

SNCF 050T D167 (0-10-0T) The chassis is from a Tri-ang 0-6-0, drilled to take five axles. The motor is at the front end. The 2nd and 5th axles have flanged wheels, the remainder unflanged. Coupling-rods made from old rails, filed flat. Cylinders and valve-gear of a fifteen-bob 3-rail Hornby Duchess from a junk-shop. The whole of the upper works is made from scrap tin, Plastikard, woods lead, etc. Painted SNCF green. Can tackle up to 15 coaches on the level.

SNCF X 4203 Autorail Panoramique More or less untouched Jouef model, except for detail improvements in the painting, and a Plastikard floor at one end to prevent the light for the head-lamps shining downwards on to the track. Fast, but very smoothly controllable, and growls noisily. But then Diesels do, don't they.

SNCF 231 E 22 (Chapelon Pacific) A Tri-ang Princess chassis, with the trailing truck replaced by one from a Dublo 0-6-2T. The valve gear is Tri-ang from the return crank to the expansion link, the rest of it is a collection of bent pins, flattened wire, etc, which took weeks of trial and error. The whole of the upperworks were made from the 'scrap drawer' of Plastikard, tin, lead, wire, balsa, electric flex covering and ball-point pen caps (for the head-lamps, for instance). Very interesting project indeed. The tender is a Jouef, modernised. Painted SNCF green, gold lining, white numbers. Fast, powerful, but not yet as smooth running as I hoped.

The latest locomotive, only just begun, is **SNCF 141 R 500,** one of the first batch of immediately post-war 2-8-2s supplied by Baldwin, USA. The tender is complete; the body came from a Stanier (Dublo) 8F and is mounted on Jouef bogies. The construction of the locomotive will be by the same method as the 0-10-0T. To be painted matt black.

All these French locomotives are contemporaries, but I doubt if any 'Panoramique' ever got within 500 miles of a Collin super-Pacific. I suppose it is a bit like having a Caledonian engine on the Brighton, but the French aspect of the layout has not yet got any geographical or historical background, however far-fetched. Any suggestions . . .

All this activity has produced one big dissatisfaction: having built up a stud of locomotives, several of which are capable of hauling trains 10ft long, it is frustrating to be more or less confined to a cupboard to watch them chasing their own tails. Someday (after retirement, perhaps?) maybe there will be a layout with a 25-foot straight run whereon a Pacific can dent the speed-limit with a full-length 'rapide'!

The Yeo Valley Railway

A OOn9 layout.

G. BARNABE

Right: *The view of Penrhyn on the Festiniog Railway shows what the station at Yeo St Anne's or Bampton Forum could look like.*

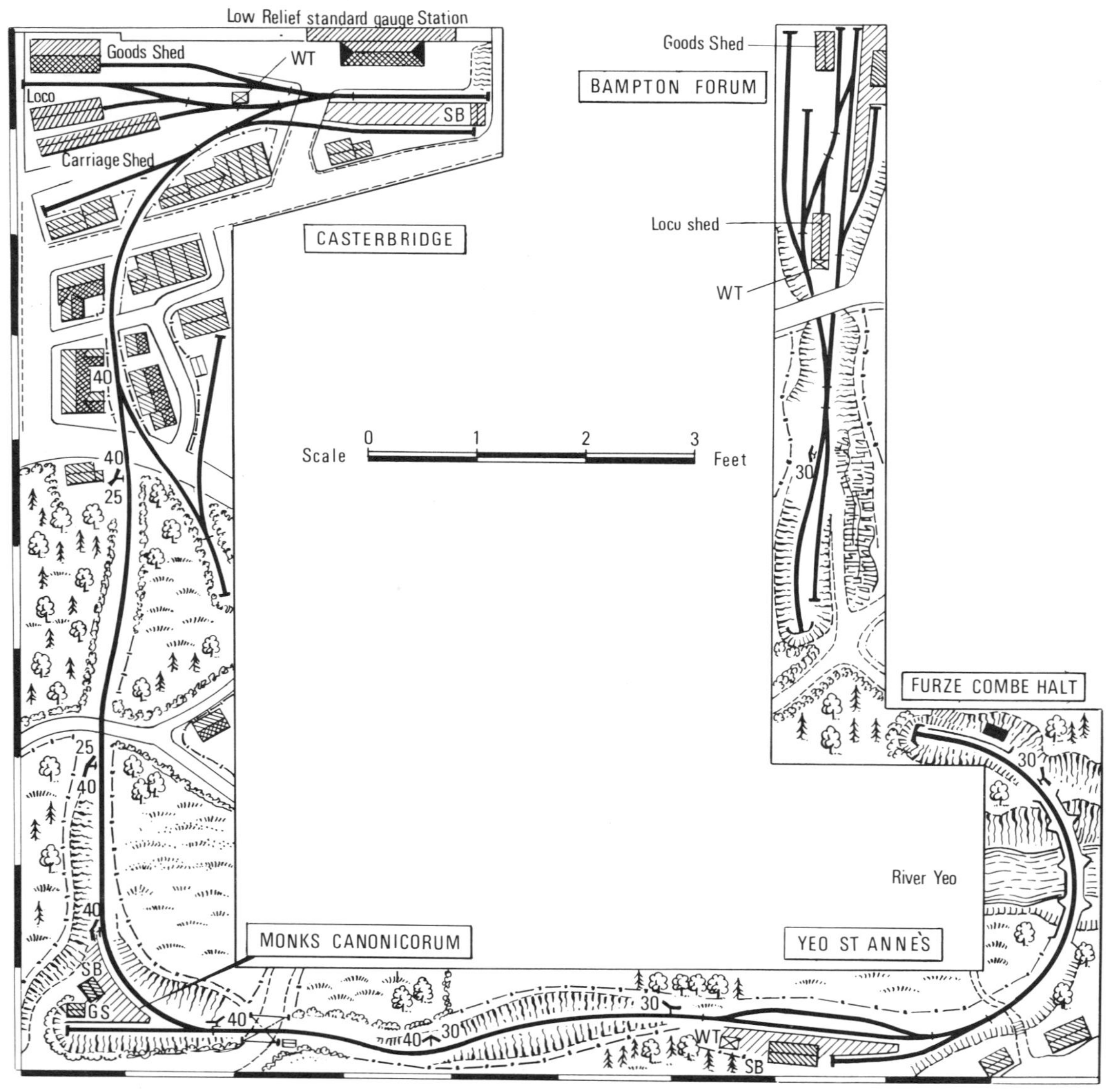

The story of the Yeo Valley — Mk1 was originally told in the *Narrow Gauge Journal* issues for May and June 1970. This 009 layout was built as a small test track to experiment with track laying techniques and to assess the running qualities of various pieces of rolling stock. Needless to say scenery was then provided and the 'test track' developed as a layout in its own right. The following is a description of the Yeo Valley — Mk2 which seems likely to succeed my present 00n3 layout. One of the attractions of 009 is that the relatively small trains seem to have further to go when travelling through model countryside, and the scenic treatment of the layout has been planned to include features taken from various n.g. lines.

The headquarters of the YVR are at Casterbridge where the terminus is situated in the forecourt of the GWR station (Welshpool & Llanfair influence). The standard gauge station could either be treated in low relief or else be represented on the backscene, in either case a Brunel timber train shed would be typical of the location and also serve the useful process of cutting down the amount of standard gauge modelling required. The NG goods yard is rather cramped and is reached by setting back from the platform. The original W&L yard was laid out differently but the main features have been retained though they have been regrouped. There is room for a corrugated iron loco shed and another similar to house the coaching stock, together with a couple of goods sidings. The line running into the goods shed and the lead from the loop are assumed to run under a road bridge at this end of the yard to an interchange siding with the GWR. Leaving the station the YVR swings across the High Street and plunges among the back yards of Casterbridge. A narrow street junction at a level crossing is an echo of Seven Stars and photos of Welshpool will be the scenic inspiration here, although the architectural styles will be a little different. Just before the line leaves the town a siding strikes out to the left, with a kick-back serving some small industry — probably a saw-mill. This is really provided as somewhere to park the odd goods wagon when the station yard is full. A gentle gradient begins among the houses, but immediately after the last road crossing it stiffens to 1 in 25. The ground at the back of the baseboard will be higher than the line, sloping down to the tracks, and thickly wooded. Below the line the slope continues down to the front of the baseboard as fields of rough pasture divided by hedges.

Still climbing the train leaves the shelter of the hedges and woods and crosses a narrow lane as the gradient slackens to 1 in 40. A shallow cutting rises on the right and Monks Canonicorum station is reached, situated on a left hand bend. There is a simple passenger shelter and at the rear of the platform is a short siding where a lock-up shed suffices as a goods store. A steep lane leads up to the cottages of the village. Leaving the station the line passes a level crossing (the only one provided with gates) and continues climbing at 1 in 40 through the fields to the first summit from where it falls at 1 in 30 through a grassy cutting to reach Yeo St Anne. This is an important station and has a loop that can be used for crossing trains when required, though usually it holds a few wagons while others are being unloaded in the goods siding. The station building bears some resemblance to Penrhyn, and there is a water tank at the Down end of the platform. Leaving the loop and skirting the village the line curves away to the left in a complete semicircle and in doing so crosses a substantial stone viaduct over the valley of the River Yeo, reminiscent of the scene at Chelfam on the Lynton & Barnstaple. The fertile lower valley is left behind and the scenery is now more rugged with gorse bushes and rocky outcrops. Following the viaduct the climb is re-started at 1 in 30 and situated on a reverse curve in a cutting is Furze Combe Halt, though the train crews try not to stop here when travelling in the Up direction unless requested. At the end of the platform the line enters a short tunnel blasted through the rock from which it emerges to run past a stone quarry before passing below an overbridge. This is journey's end, the line is once more level as the run-round loop at Bampton Forum opens up. The station has two platform faces and plenty of siding accommodation for goods traffic. There is also a small loco shed incorporating the water tower and it is here that the 'top shunter' is shedded. The market town of Bampton is represented on the backscene.

Rolling stock will be commercially available items modified to represent, or at least suggest, British prototypes. For instance the Playcraft tramway bogie coach can, with a minimum of surgery, be converted to a 'shorty' Welshpool type coach, and similarly there would seem to be possibilities with the Thommen 0-6-0T produced by Liliput. Goods stock should present little trouble, bearing in mind that most British lines seemed to favour small four-wheeled wagons, with only a few exceptions. Indeed, using Plasikard and N gauge wagon underframes (available separately) almost any prototype could be quickly and cheaply constructed. Above all I have tried to create the basis of a layout interesting to build as well as operate, and where trains will have to be really *driven,* possibly with the aid of weight-simulation.

Below: *'Leaving the station the YVR plunges among the back yards of Casterbridge'. A somewhat similar situation on the town section (now abandoned) of the Welshpool & Llanfair Railway. The line is on the far side of the rubble in the foreground.*

Right: *A view of 'Seven Stars' Welshpool as it is today. This ran behind the ruins to the left (once a picturesque half timbered cottage) before crossing the road junction behind the parked cars.*

Below right: *The level crossing at Castle Caereinion provides a prototype for the setting of Monks Canonicorum.*

STOP
5

Right: *The railway approach to Seven Stars on the Welshpool-Llanfair. Part of the timber beams of the cottage can be seen. The building was demolished as unsafe after the Sylfaen Brook (in a culvert below the track) flooded a few years ago.*

Below: *'Leaving the station, the YVR swings across the High Street at Casterbridge'. This view shows Church Street in Welshpool. The W&L once ran between high stone walls behind the chain link fence before crossing the road and squeezing between the houses by the first lamp post on the left of the illustration.*

Vintage Items

A glimpse at some of the crude 'toytrains' of yesteryear should make some of the critics of today's proprietary items bite their tongues! It shows how the model railway hobby has progressed and how discerning the enthusiast has become.

Below: *Believed to be a Bassett-Lowke made 2½in gauge steam model of a SECR 4-4-0. c1903.*

Bottom: *A supposedly well detailed gauge 2 model of a Bavarian 4-4-0 with the usual clockwork propulsion made by Bing c1900.*

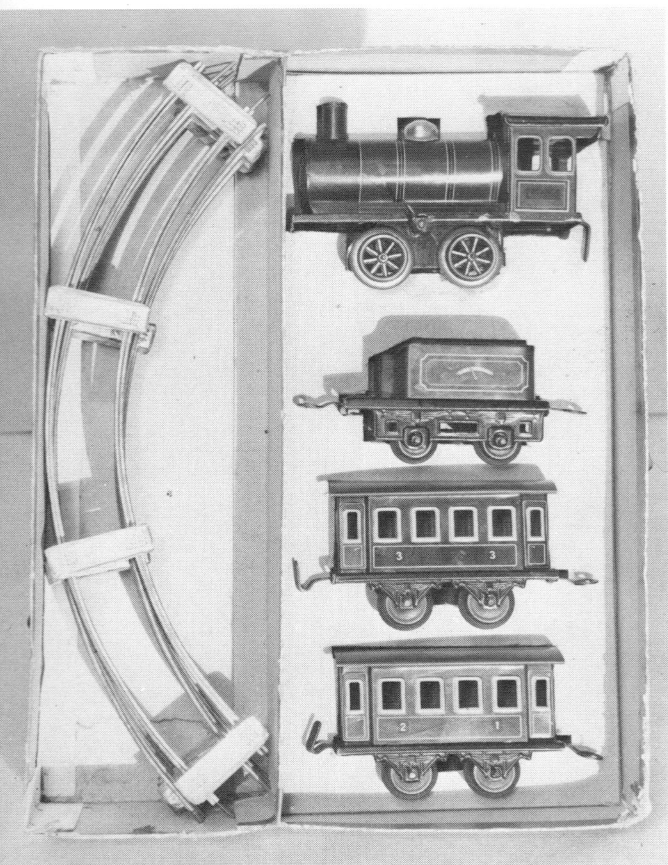

Above: *A Hornby O gauge No 2 tank loco. This 4-4-2 chassis and body was available for LMSR, LNER, GWR and SR and only the colour of the paint and the number differed! It was extremely popular in the mid-1920s. This version is clockwork and the two rods projecting from the cab enabled the operator to start/stop and engage forward/reverse.*

Left: *A gauge O train set as made by the German firm of Bing in 1908.*

Below: *Two gauge O tinplate trains of their period. A clockwork MR 4-2-2 with two clerestory coaches and a LBSCR 4-4-2T, also clockwork, although standing on Hornby O gauge tinplate track* / Great Western Society

Right: *A French JEP gauge O model electric loco and two open wagons of the early 1930s.*

Below right: *A very early electric model loco now worth considerably more than its price when new!*

0-35

A Continental Miscellany

Below: *A Jouef model of the SNCF 231K class on the layout of Nick Wood — again a normal French model and run straight out of the box with no modification.* / Brian Monaghan

Bottom: *A Rivarossi HO scale (3.5mm:1ft) model of the SNCF 231E class Pacific bursts out of a tunnel on the Clochmerle-en-Beaujolais (SNCF) layout of Nick Wood. This illustration clearly shows the amount of detail on the model, which is a standard proprietary item.* / Brian Monaghan

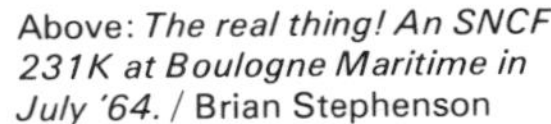

Above: *The real thing! An SNCF 231K at Boulogne Maritime in July '64.* / Brian Stephenson

Top left: *The new SNCF double deck suburban coaches.* / Railphot, Y. Broncard

Centre left: *The Jouef models of the double deck suburban coaches behind a Class BB 17000 electric loco.*

Bottom left: *A cosmopolitan array of electric locomotives in N gauge by Arnold and all will work from either the two rails or from the overhead catenary. Furthest from camera is a German type 94 as used by the Austrian State Railways (OBB), in the centre is the DB type 141, and nearest the camera an SNCF type 7100.* / Arnold

Above: *A scene on the HO scale German layout named 'Ruritania' owned and operated by Roland Balderstone. This view is of the mpd at the end of the station, and left to right the locos are — Class 80 0-6-0T and Class 55, 0-8-0 both Fleischmann models; the next road is a Class 65, while entering the station is an OBB (Austrian) Class 638 loco with a semi-fast train which is passing an outgoing local headed by a Class 70 loco. A DB Class 44 2-10-0 is on the spur road near the tunnel mouth* / Brian Monaghan

Right: *Many HO scale layouts feature an N gauge section and the 'Ruritania' layout of Roland Balderstone shown here is no exception. This HOn9 train runs from somewhere up the mountains down to the main station and alongside its big brothers, and such arrangements can be seen in the prototype.* / Brian Monaghan

Left: *A scene on the N gauge layout of Frank Wilkinson which mainly follows German practice. The main line runs on the embankment while the branch line runs alongside the river. The 'old-time' branch train represents a preserved line and is a Fleischmann model.*
/ Brian Monaghan

Below: *Trams are a common sight on the Continent and many HO scale layouts will feature a working tramway system. These are manufactured by several concerns such as Hamo and those shown here by Mehanotechnica which are more of the American Birnie car but capable of conversion and they are economically priced.*

Right: *A DB shunting and branch line diesel loco type 290. Models of this and similar diesel locos are made by many of the manufacturers in both HO and N scales.*

Below: *A model railway in Germany portraying the scene near Altenbeken. This shows the approach to the main station. Most of the locomotives and rolling stock are correctly weathered and the whole has a most realistic appearance.*
/ Rolf Ertmer

Modellers Metallurgy

V. A. CALLCUT

Most model constructors turn their hands to the use of metal in some form or other, the advantages being the durability and effective weight of the finished article.

In using metal the modeller is dabbling in what has been called 'the oldest of arts but youngest of sciences'. For those who know little or nothing of metallurgy the following notes give a brief background to some of the common terms used in our hobby and an explanation of some of the processes used.

Alloy A mixture of any two or more metals. All commercial alloys are made to achieve properties not possible with pure metals.

Aluminium A metal popular elsewhere but little used by modellers because it is difficult to solder and its light weight is not required, except possibly for the bodies of coaches.

Annealing Heating a metal to soften it by removing the strains caused by cold work. Subsequent quenching is not essential but may be used to help remove oxide scale. For both mild steel and copper a dull red heat is adequate while brass and aluminium need lower temperatures. In each case the time needed is dependent on metal size: heavy sections need longer than thin ones. Excessive heating of most metals causes embrittlement.

Anodising Aluminium Has a hard dense oxide film formed on it by immersion in a sulphuric acid electrolyte. Chemicals may be included to colour the film which is to a certain extent electrically insulating.

Babbit Metal A range of tin — lead — copper — antimony alloys used for whitemetal bearings.

Brass Alloys of copper and zinc for a great variety of uses requiring good corrosion resistance and easy working and solderability. Typically brass for castings or hot forgings has 60% copper while that for cold working in sheet or wire form has 63-70% copper. Brass in rod form may have 2% lead added to give it 'free machinability'. In this form it may be bent cold after annealing if necessary, but will crack if bent hot. There are several brasses with special additions made to give higher strength and even better corrosion resistance.

Brazing A medium temperature joining technique giving joints intermediate in strength between soft soldering and welding. It is suitable for copper and steel and, with care, brass. The earliest brazing spelter was a 50/50 copper zinc alloy but the manufacturers now have many varieties available to suit various requirements. The addition of silver gives a more expensive filler with a lower melting temperature and much greater fluidity. Because of this fluidity joint gaps for silver soldering should be smaller than for higher temperature brazing. For most brazing a suitable flux is required.

Bronze Any alloy which is mainly copper. Commonly this means a copper-tin-phosphorus alloy also known as phosphor bronze containing 3 to 10% tin. For a copper alloy this has a high strength and hardness combined with the usual corrosion resistance. It can be cast into sticks or rod suitable for machining to make bearings ideal for supporting hard steel shafts at high speed. Another type can be cold rolled down very thin and hard to make an easily soldered springy metal ideal for electrical pickups and contacts.

Aluminium bronze is usually used as cast for applications requiring resistance to sea-water corrosion; it is difficult to solder because of the aluminium content. Manganese bronze is a high tensile brass capable of strengths over 30 tonf/in^2. Neither of these is much use to modellers.

Case Hardening See Mild Steel.

Cast Iron Iron containing 2-4% carbon has a lower melting point than steel and when poured is very fluid, taking the shape of complex moulds easily. Common cast iron is very hard and brittle and not suitable for any further work but many varieties are produced to meet special needs. By extra alloying additions or heat treatments malleable metal may be produced but it remains unsuitable for small models. There will be plenty of cast iron in most workshops however, in the vice, and forming the heavy bases of most machine tools.

Copper Usually thought of as a soft ductile metal with a characteristic colour kept only by frequent polishing, copper finds frequent use where its high conductivity for electricity or heat is required. It has good corrosion resistance and is easily soldered. Normally it is not easy to cut or machine as it clogs saw teeth and drills. Free machining copper is made but its use is generally restricted by the fact that some of the good properties are lost — the usual answers are to use coarse saw blades or stop drilling to clean the bit frequently.

Most copper is 'tough pitch' and has oxygen dissolved in it. For most applications this is ideal but the reducing gases like hydrogen, found in hot flames, can attack this oxygen, forming steam which expands and embrittles or 'gases' the copper internally. For large fireboxes, components needing extended torch brazing, or for the bits of flame heated soldering irons deoxidised copper is used to avoid this trouble. Special clear laquers such as Incralac are now available to keep copper bright.

Corrosion When exposed to air and dampness most metals oxidise and lose their bright metallic lustre. Only one or two metals like gold and platinum are relatively immune and the prices of these reflect that important point! Many chemists and metallurgists are devoting their efforts towards cheaper protection and are evolving a variety of ideas.

Note the general need for both air and dampness: in very dry air or immersed in pure water boiled free of dissolved oxygen, corrosion rates are much reduced. The most severe corrosion is found in damp air or where metal is repeatedly wetted rather than continually immersed in water.

If corrosion of any metal is a problem the following general suggestions may be considered:

1. Keep dry.
2. Smear with grease or oil.
3. Coat with another metal, ie plate or galvanise.
4. Coat with suitable paint or lacquer recommended to give good protection.
5. Use a vapour phase inhibitor protective paper as suggested by the manufacturers.
6. Avoid contact between certain dissimilar metals in damp or wet conditions ie iron can rust very quickly if in contact with copper.

Crystallisation All metals are crystalline as solidified, a structure which can be seen after polishing and etching a specimen or at fractures. It is best seen after fracture of a brittle material rather than a ductile one.

Die Casting The process of solidifying metal in moulds which give an exact replica of the part required. These reusable moulds are normally made of hard metal and open in several directions to enable complex shapes to be made. The metal may be poured in (gravity die cast) or pumped in to the die to get better filling (pressure die cast).

Frequently the metal used is a zinc — 4% aluminium alloy which is fluid enough when molten to get into complex dies and has reasonable strength when solid. It melts at a fairly low temperature but even so the dies must be robust and are therefore expensive to make in tough steel. The process is only economic when long production runs are possible.

Some early diecasting alloys were impure and very sensitive to internal corrosion in damp atmospheres. This resulted in an apparently perfect part suddenly

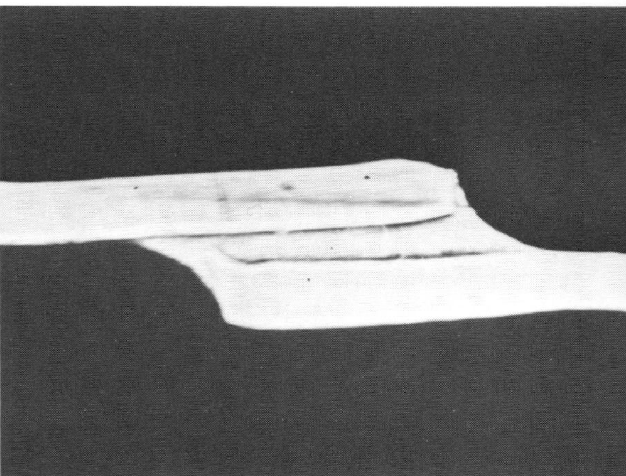

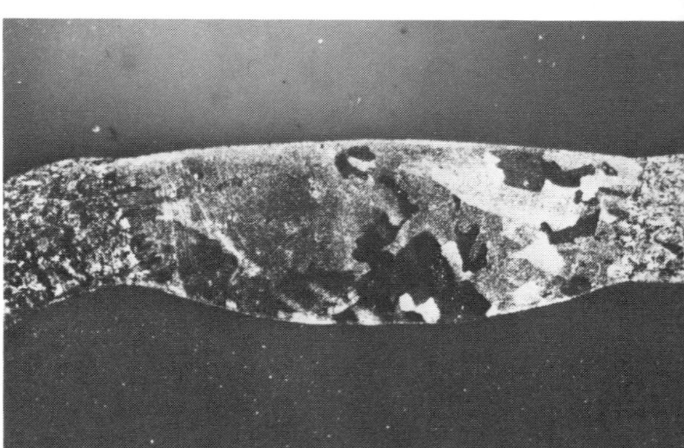

Top: *Section through a seam joint in a commercial tin can. A good joint economically soldered. Tin coating on the steel too thin to be seen at this magnification. (Mag x 10).* / M. W. Vandy

Centre: *Section through a silver soldered lap joint. Well 'wetted' but no alloying between sheet and filler (Mag x 10).* / M. W. Vandy

Above: *Section through a weld in 76thou thick copper etched to show full alloying in the joint. (Mag x 14).* / M. W. Vandy

crumbling under the slightest stress. Modern components are not so susceptible, being made from better alloys.

For short runs cheaper dies are essential and so the metal used has a lower melting temperature. Whitemetal kits for modellers are made this way with many intricate components in each one. This metal is expensive but ideal for the job.

Fatigue Repeated stresses will often break a metal even when less than the strength of the metal itself. A small fracture starts at some crack or sharp indentation and this propagates slowly across until fracture occurs. The effect depends on the stress, the number of applications and the sensitivity of the metal to nicks caused by such things as sharp machining grooves or other 'stress raisers'. It can usually be avoided by careful design and machining. It can also be very useful when you have cut part way through a piece of metal, to waggle it about until the last bit just breaks off!

Fluxes Most of the soldering, brazing and welding methods need clean metal to ensure a sound joint. Once heat is applied most metals oxidise and the filler metal may not then wet the joint properly. The basic job of a flux is to cover the prepared joint to prevent oxidation at the operating temperature. Most of them are also 'active' in removing any slight oxidation that has taken place.

Many fluxes have been prepared to suit various metals and jointing techniques and temperatures. The correct one must always be used to ensure success. Some active fluxes tend to be corrosive and joints should generally be cleaned after having been made.

Galvanising Steel is a relatively cheap and strong structural metal but it does rust very quickly if left unprotected. If clean sheet is dipped through a flux into molten zinc an alloy layer is formed which is ideal for this purpose. The coating is sacrificial, which means that even if it is perforated or broken afterwards such as by sawing, it still restricts the corrosion of the steel underneath. The spangles seen on galvanised sheet are very thin crystals of zinc formed as it solidifies on cooling.

Gunmetals A range of strong copper base alloys used as high strength forgings and castings and usually containing additions to tin, zinc and lead. These machine well but are not suitable for cold bending.

Heat Treatment This term usually refers to the hardening and tempering of carbon steels but the properties of many alloys can be improved by specified heating, quenching and reheating to lower temperatures.

Lost Wax (Cire Perdue) Investment Casting A process developed in mediaeval times for the production of castings with intricate shapes to a high precision. A wax replica of the part required is first made. This is then coated with a fine refractory cement which sets round it. After warming in an oven to run out the wax an accurate mould is left. This is then fired at high temperature to burn off any residual wax before the required metal is run in. The mould must be broken to get the solidified casting out and a new one made for each cast required, which explains the fairly high production cost, but the technique can be used for metals of any melting point including brass, nickel silver and stainless steel.

Melting Temperatures of Modellers' Metals

	°C	*°F (approx)*
Woods Metal Low melting point solder	70	160
Kit Whitemetal (Cerrocast)	140-170	280-340
Tin-lead solder 60/40	183	360
40/60	183-230	360-450
Tin	231	450
Lead	327	620
Diecasting Zinc (4% aluminium)	385	725
Silver Solder (Easiflo No 2)	608-617	1130-1140
Brazing Alloys	650-830	1200-1530
Aluminium	660	1220
Brass	900-950	1650-1740
Nickel Silver	about 1050	about 1920
Copper	1083	1980
Cast Iron	about 1100	about 2000
Steel	about 1400	about 2550

Melting Point The temperature at which a pure metal turns from solid to liquid. Most alloys usually do this over a range of temperature, going through a pasty half-liquid, half-solid state.

Mould The container in which liquid metal is solidified to a required shape. It may be of suitable metal, bonded sand or even plaster, depending on the casting required. The mould must be strong at the casting temperature and able to conduct heat away fast. It should be made with a taper to allow pattern and metal removal and may be slightly oversize to allow for contraction on solidification and cooling. To avoid spitting when the metal is poured moulds must be dry — plaster moulds especially should be oven dried.

Nickel Silver (German Silver) A brass with about 12% nickel added to improve strength and corrosion resistance. It contains no silver at all.

Pewter 71 to 78% tin, remainder lead. A malleable sheet metal neglected by modellers except when made into tankards.

Plating The deposition of one metal on another in an electrolytic bath. The electrolyte is a solution of various salts and may be alkaline or acid according to requirements. DC current is passed from an immersed electrode called an anode to the item to be plated which forms the cathode. On arrival it deposits metal in a thin uniform layer.

Above: *Phosphor-bronze cold rolled 50% and etched to show distorted fibrous crystal structure. (Mag × 300).* / *Copper Development Assoc*

Below: *Phosphor-bronze as above after annealing. Uniform crystal structure. (Mag × 300).* / Copper Development Assoc

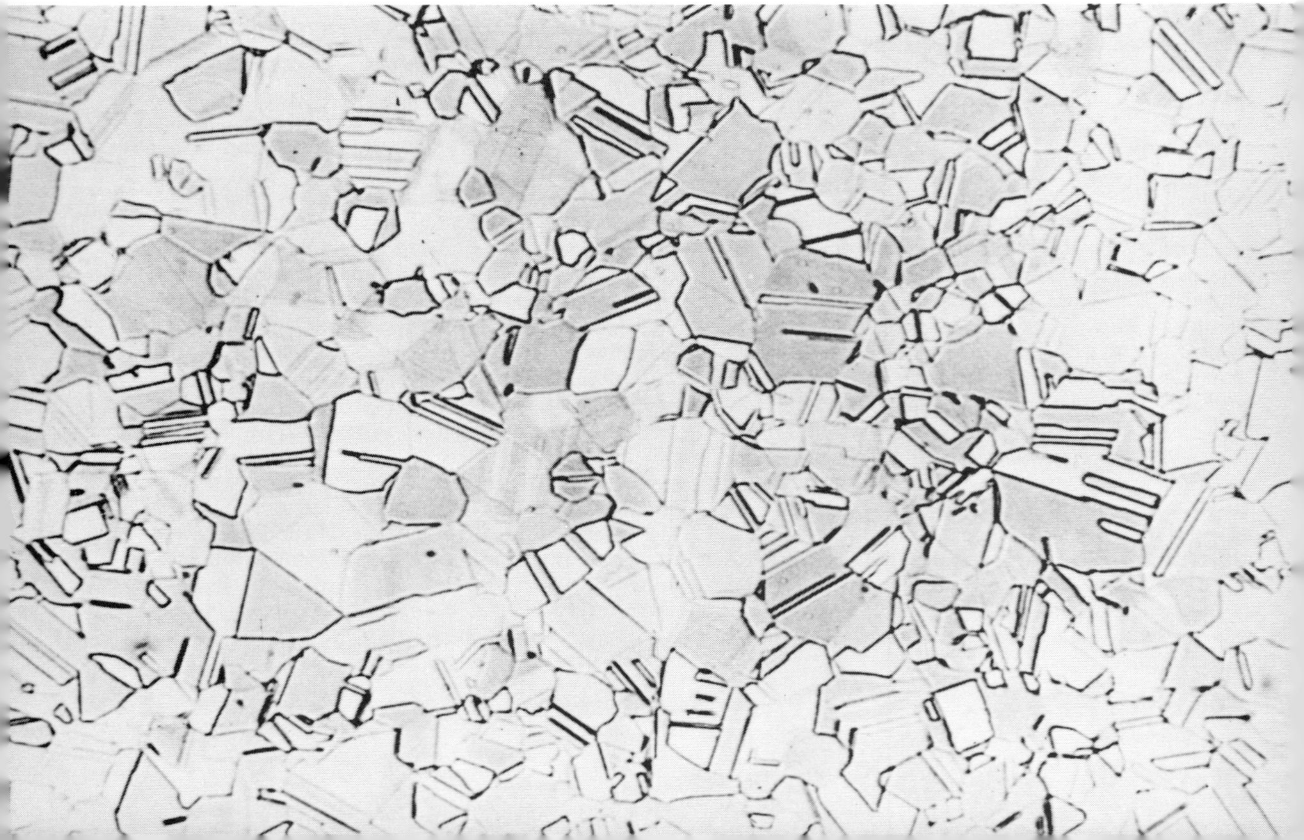

Chromium plating usually consists of a 0.00001in flash of chromium on top of a 0.001-0.0001in nickel undercoat, the reason for this being that chrome is hard and bright but the nickel is needed for durability. If the plating is on steel a copper flush is needed under the nickel to get a good bond.

Powder Metallurgy Fine metal powders may be compacted and heated so that they bond together to make solid metal. Many metals can be treated this way for a wide variety of uses. Intricate shapes may be made similar to castings if the powder is pressed in to shaped dies and the process is sometimes competitive with diecasting: some driving wheels are made this way.

By careful pressing of the powders the porosity of the final compact may be controlled so that for example sintered bronze bearings may be left porous to retain oil better.

Steel is an alloy of iron and carbon, there being much less carbon than in cast iron. As mild steel it has 0.1-0.2% which helps to make it a very useful and comparatively cheap ductile structural material. Black mild steel is sold as hot rolled with some millscale still adherent. For a cleaner surface and better conformance to size ask for bright mild steel. This has been cold rolled to size and annealed without scaling.

Mild steel cannot be hardened by simple heat treatment. A higher carbon content is needed and it is usual to have other small alloying additions. Silver steel (designated EN 31) commonly has 1.1% carbon, 0.35% manganese and 0.2%silicon and can be hardened by the usual process of heating to cherry red heat (800-840°C) followed by a quick quench in water. Tempering is carried out by reheating until a cleaned part of the component has turned the required colour. Light straw (at 130-180°C) means a hard brittle steel; this may be varied through to a dark blue (at 300°C) which gives a softer but tougher metal.

The carbon content of the surface of mild steel can be raised during case hardening so that it can then be hardened and tempered like a high carbon steel to form a hard outside on a ductile mild steel centre. For the modeller who has no access to a cyanide salt bath the best way to effect this is to bury the component in a tin of Casenit or other hardening compound and seal the lid with clay or refractory cement before baking to cherry red heat for some time. The old method of dip-coating metal with compound and repeatedly returning it to a bright red heat is usually limited in its usefulness by the fact that unless the metal is well surrounded by red hot coke any carbon will be oxidised away again as soon as it is formed.

Stainless steel is highly alloyed iron, having usually 18% nickel, 8% chromium and a price which reflects the increased difficulty in melting and working the stuff as well as the extra cost of the alloying additions. This 'austenitic' steel has a very high resistance to corrosion and is not magnetic, unlike the cheaper stainless iron (12% chromium, no nickel) which has slightly less stain resistance.

Soldering involves wetting adjacent metals with a liquid metal of lower melting point which then freezes to give a permanent joint. No alloying takes place and the joint strength is limited to the strength of the solder or its bond to the metals being joined, whichever is the lower. Brass, copper or steel may easily be soldered with common tin/lead solder provided they are clean and are kept that way by flux during the joining. Aluminium and some of its alloys may be soldered to each other with special solder and flux but not easily to other metals. From the table of melting temperatures it can be seen why it is necessary to use a special low melting point solder for kit whitemetals.

Symbols The metallurgists among the early Greeks chose symbols to represent each metal rather than the chemical abbreviations used today. If you see a tie about, decorated with o and o symbols it is as well to know they are the Greek signs for iron and copper and the tie belongs to a member of the Institution of Metallurgists.

Tin cans Most of these invaluable food containers are made of thin steel sheet coated with a much thinner layer of tin metal to give a cheap malleable, solderable raw material for modellers. Formerly a good thickness of tin was applied by dipping the steel into a fluxed tin bath but now the thickness of tin is kept to a minimum and may be applied by dipping or electroplating. The tin thickness is kept so thin that cans are now frequently lacquered internally to give extra protection and this reduces solderability slightly. Unlike galvanising the tin coating is not sacrificial. Once penetrated the steel underneath may rust freely.

Welding If the edges of two adjacent metals are just melted they will fuse together, forming a weld. Normally a filler metal is fed in to the molten weld pool as it progresses along the joint and the use of a suitable flux to prevent excessive oxidation is usual. It is possible for welds in many materials to be as strong and ductile as the parent metal.

Whitemetal is a term commonly including all alloys of fairly low melting points including the babbitts used for bearings and typemetals. To the modeller it now means that fairly expensive tin-bismuth alloy which can be cast easily to good replicas of complex shapes and is extremely ductile for a cast metal.

Woodsmetal A bismuth-lead-tin-cadmium alloy melting at 70°C which used to be known for its use for joke spoons which melted in hot tea, but is now of greater service for soldering kit whitemetals.